BERKSHIRE VICTUALS

Janet Pearce Cook, *Editor*

The Berkshire County Historical Society — Arrowhead

> The greatest pleasure may be taken, by the philosopher and naturalist (and the farmer should be both) in contemplating that benign process by which ingredients the most offensive to the human senses are converted into articles that gratify the most delicate taste, and pamper the most luxurious appetite.
>
> **HERMAN MELVILLE,**
> *REPORT OF THE COMMITTEE ON AGRICULTURE (1850)*

BERKSHIRE COUNTY HISTORICAL SOCIETY

This effort is dedicated to the memory of
Richard Seitz   President BCHS
Mary Combes   Faithful Member and Worker

Berkshire Victuals
Copyright © 1993, The Berkshire County Historical Society
All rights reserved. Duplication of material (except items reprinted with permission) allowable with credit to The Berkshire County Historical Society, 780 Holmes Road, Pittsfield, MA 01201 (413) 442-1793. Additional copies available by mail order from the publisher.

Cook, Janet Pearce
Berkshire Victuals, Berkshire County Historical Society
ISBN 0-9639206-0-X

Printed in U.S.A. The Berkshire Eagle Publishing Company

WITHIN

		Page
FRONTSPIECE APPETIZERS	Old Sources	1
	Contemporary Sources	8
TITLE PAGE SOUPS	Old Sources	14
	Contemporary Sources	19
FOREWORD EGGS CHEESE PASTA RICE BEANS	Old Sources	25
	Contemporary Sources	32
PREFACE BREAD BREAKFAST	Old Sources	40
	Contemporary Sources	50
TABLE OF CONTENTS:		
BOOK I SEAFOOD	Old Sources	56
	Contemporary Sources	66
BOOK II POULTRY	Old Sources	71
	Contemporary Sources	77
BOOK III MEAT	Old Sources	86
	Contemporary Sources	95
BOOK IV VEGETABLES SALADS	Old Sources	103
	Contemporary Sources	110
BOOK V COOKIES CAKES PIES	Old Sources	118
	Contemporary Sources	130
ADDENDA SAUCES RELISHES CONDIMENTS	Old Sources	143
	Contemporary Sources	154
EPILOGUE PUDDINGS DESSERTS CONFECTIONS	Old Sources	161
	Contemporary Sources	175
FINIS BEVERAGES	Old Sources	179
	Contemporary Sources	192
VINTAGE CAUTIONS & PRECAUTIONS		194

BLENDINGS

In the universal hunt for things ancestral, one essential part of the old life has been neglected. Why should empty platters and plates be cherished as something sacred while the contents for which alone they existed are forgotten?

Surely a dish of victuals had a closer connection with a grandfather than a dish of Canton china. In a sense, the victual was itself an ancestor. The blood it fed still flows in living veins. Then let it be honored and its history told.[1]

In 1962 a group of Berkshire County citizens organized to celebrate their roots. The geography, the connection with America's past history, the concentration of lettered people have proved fertile material for a foray into our past. The historical society continues to make connections between the present and past, acknowledging our debts in both directions.

Janet P. Cook

HERMAN MELVILLE

One of the lettered men is of special interest because his home, Arrowhead, is the headquarters of the historical society. Here the time of Bryant, Hawthorne, Wharton, Holmes and Melville blend into the present and come together with the best ingredients, old and new. In this cooperative spirit we present the recipes from long ago, and the contributions from current cooks.

Contemporary recipes have been tested by the donors. With old sources and historic recipes, proceed at your own risk.

Enclosed in boxes are authentic authors of family recipes. Boxed recipes are from authentic family recipes.

The general rather than the specific directions from old sources presents a problem to the cook. Variations in spelling and punctuation are replicated from original sources as cited. In contemporary recipes author directions are as submitted.

FRONTISPIECE APPETIZERS OLD SOURCES

Try some plump alderman, and suck the blood
Enriched by generous wine and costly meat;
On well-filled skins, sleek as they native mud,
Fix they light pump and press they freckled feet.
Go to the men for whom, in ocean's halls,
The oyster breeds, and the green turtle sprawls.

WILLIAM CULLEN BRYANT,
TO A MOSQUITO

In the long try watches of the night, it is a common thing for the seamen to dip their ship-biscuit into the huge oil-pots and let them fry there awhile. Many a good supper have I thus made.

HERMAN MELVILLE, *MOBY-DICK*

TO DRESS CRAB

Ingredients
1 crab, 2 tablespoons of vinegar, 1 ditto of oil; salt, white pepper, and cayenne, to taste.

Mode
Empty the shells, and thoroughly mix the meat with the above ingredients, and put it in the large shell. Garnish with slices of cut lemon and parsley. The quantity of oil may be increased when it is much liked.

Average cost, from 10d to 2s.

Seasonable all the year; but not so good in May, June, and July.

Sufficient for 3 persons.

To Choose Crab
The middle-sized crab is the best; and the crab, like the lobster, should be judged by its weight; for if light, it is watery.[18]

HOT CRAB

Ingredients
1 crab, nutmeg, salt, and pepper to taste, 3 oz. of butter, ¼ lb. of bread crumbs, 3 tablespoons of vinegar.

Mode
After having boiled the crab, pick the meat out from the shells, and mix with it the nutmeg and seasoning. Cut up the butter in small pieces, and add the bread crumbs and vinegar. Mix altogether, put the whole in the large shell, and brown before the fire or in a salamander.

Time
1 hour. Average cost, from 10d to 2s. Seasonable all the year; but not so good in May, June, and July. Sufficient for 3 persons.[18]

THE CRAB TRIBE - The whole of this tribe of animals have the body covered with a hard and strong shell, and they live chiefly in the sea. [18]

DUNBAR SHRIMPS
Mrs. Walter Hall

Put large lump of butter in pan with salt, cayenne, 1½ teaspoons tablesauce and 2 cups cream, when hot add 2 hard-boiled eggs chopped fine and 1 pint shrimp chopped fine; let them come to a boil. Serve on hot dainty potato chips or toast. [12]

DEVILED CLAMS
Mrs. Walter Hall

Chop 50 clams very fine; take 2 tomatoes, 1 onion chopped fine, a little parsley, sweet butter, little salt, pepper, bread crumbs, adding juice of clams, until mixture is consistency of sausage; put in shells (quohaug shells) with lump of butter on each; cover with bread crumbs, and bake ½ hour. [12]

For the Flying Rheumatism.
Prince's pine tops, horseradish roots, elecampane roots, prickly ash bark, bittersweet bark off the roots, wild cherry bark and mustard seed, a small handful of each; one gill of tar water into one pint of brandy, or in that proportion. Drink a small glass before eating three times a day. [1]

Dry Sweet Flag-Root grated and mixed with sugar, cures colic in babies. [1]

TIMBALES

Timbales are forms of pastry or of forcemeat filled with salpicon. They are made in individual, border, or cylinder molds. The receipts below give the rules for making the pastry, forcemeat, and salpicon, and the combinations. For forcemeats, the raw meat is used, and may be used alone or mixed with panada: in the latter case it is called Quenelle forcemeat. Cut the meat or fish in pieces (excepting chicken, which is scraped), and pound it in a mortar to separate the flesh from the fiber, then press it through a puree sieve. Do not chop the meat, as the fiber is not then so easily separated. If the meat pulp is mixed with panada, press it through the sieve again so the paste will be perfectly smooth and fine. Truffles are used in decorating the molds and in the salpicon. The little bits left from the decoration are chopped and used in the salpicon stuffing for beef, veal, or mutton or in a sauce. [16]

TIMBALES Á l'ECOSSAUSE

Butter well six small timbale molds, and line them with cuts of plain, unsweetened pancake. Take a preparation of puree of chicken, and the same quantity of raw forcemeat, add to it a reduced salpicon, and with this fill molds. Cover with small round pieces of the pancake. Then steam them in a moderate oven for eight minutes. Unfold, dress them on a hot dish, pour a gill of hot Madeira sauce over, and serve. [14]

TIMBALES DE NOUILLES A' LA GENOISE

Sprinkle the insides of six well-buttered timbale-molds with grated, fresh bread-crumbs; line them with thin foundation paste, and fill with finely shred, boiled nouilles, adding an ounce of good butter, and seasoning with half a pinch each of salt and pepper, and the third of a pinch of nutmeg; also half a pinch each of salt and pepper, and the third of a pinch of nutmeg; also half an ounce of grated Parmesan cheese. Thicken with a gill of strong Madeira sauce. Cover the molds with pieces of the foundation paste, and put them into a brisk oven for six minutes. Unmold, and arrange them on a hot dish containing a gill of hot Madeira sauce and with the timbales on top. [14]

It has been said that "what appeals to the eye generally appeals to the palate." [4]

Use care and taste in serving; dainty service will make the simplest food most attractive. [4]

SALPICON OF LOBSTER, CRAWFISH, OR SHRIMPS

Put a pint of béchamel into a saucepan, with four mushrooms, one truffle, and the meat from the claw of a cooked lobster, cutting them all into dice-shaped pieces. Thicken well and let cook for five minutes, and serve. If a lobster cannot be obtained, the meat of three cooked crawfish, or of six prawns or shrimps may be used instead. [14]

SALPICON Á LA MONTGLAS

Mince, as for a julienne, four mushrooms, one truffle, the breast of a small cooked chicken, or of any game, and half an ounce of cooked ham, or the same quantity of cooked, smoked beef-tongue. Put all into a saucepan, adding a gill of well reduced Madeira sauce, let cook for five minutes; then use when needed. [14]

SALPICON, SAUCE MADÉRE

Place half an ounce of good butter in a saucepan, adding half a glassful of sherry wine, a blanched throat sweetbread, nicely cut into dice-shaped pieces, four mushrooms, one truffle, and an ounce of cooked, smoked beef-tongue, all cut the same as the sweetbread. Let cook for five minutes, then add half a pint of Madeira sauce, and let cook again for five minutes. It will now be ready to use for the desired garnishing. [14]

CANAPÉ MADISON

Prepare six medium-sized slices of bread, the same shape. Toast them to a good golden color and lay them on a dish. Cover each toast with a very thin slice of lean, cooked ham; spread a little mustard over; then cover with a layer of garnishing á lá provencale, dredge grated Parmesan cheese on top, and strew a little fresh bread-crumbs over all. Place them in the hot oven and bake for ten minutes; remove, dress them on a hot dish with a folded napkin; and send to the table. [14]

CAVIARE ON TOAST

Prepare six toasts of American bread. Put half the contents of a small box of Russian caviare into a sautoire; add two tablespoons of cream, and beat one and half minutes on the stove, stirring it carefully meanwhile; pour this over the toasts, and serve on a dish with a folded napkin. [14]

LAMB SWEETBREADS EN PETITES CAISSES

Blanch, pare, and clean six small lamb sweetbreads. Lay them aside to cool, then lard them, with either fresh fat pork or truffles. Place them in a well buttered sautoire, adding a gill of chicken broth or a gill of Madeira wine. Cover with a buttered paper, and let cook to a golden color in the oven for ten minutes. Then lay them on a dish. Put half a gill of cooked fine herbs and a gill of well-reduced Espagnole sauce into the sautoire, letting it cook for five minutes. Take six small boxes of buttered paper and pour a little of the gravy at the bottom of each; cover with sweetbreads, and place them on a baking-dish; keep them for five minutes in an open oven, then serve on a folded napkin. [14]

SMALL HOT PATTIES Á L'ANGLAISE

Line with fine paté-foucer six small, hot patty-molds, fluted, and provided with hinges. Pinch the tops and fill them with common flour. Bake in a moderate oven for fifteen minutes; empty them, and leave them to dry at the oven door for five minutes. Fill them with a pint of hot salpicon royal, place a slice of truffle on the top of each instead of a cover, and serve on a hot dish with a folded napkin. [14]

SCALLOP FRITTERS
Mrs. Walter Hall

Wash and drain 1 qt. scallops, season with salt and pepper, mix with following batter: 1 pint sifted flour, scant ½ pint milk, 1 tablespoon, melted butter, 1 teaspoon salt, 2 eggs. Beat eggs briskly, add milk. Beat again and pour mixture on flour. Then add butter and salt. Stir in scallops. Drop spoonful at a time of mixture into boiling fat. Cook a nice brown. Drain on brown paper and serve very hot. [12]

Never allow any food which looks unsightly to be served. Toasted bread, burned on one side, may take away the appetite, but toasted a golden brown on both sides, with crusts cut off and then cut in strips and served in between the folds of a fresh doily, will appeal to the most fastidious. [16]

Parsley is always used to garnish meats. [4]

CHEESE STRAWS

Mix with one cupful of flour one half cupful of grated Parmesan cheese, a dash of cayenne, one half teaspoonful of salt, and the yolk of one egg; then add enough water to make a paste sufficiently consistent to roll. Place it on a board and roll to one quarter inch thickness. Cut it into narrow strips and roll so each piece will be the size and length of a lead pencil. Place them in a baking-tin and press each end on the pan so that they will not contract. Bake to a light brown in a moderate oven. Serve with salad. These straws will keep for several days, and should be heated just before serving. [16]

ONION RAREBIT

Boil and chop fine one quart onions, cream as for the table; put them into chafing dish and add one-third quantity of fresh American cheese. Let this dissolve slowly into the onion. [8]

PIGS IN BLANKETS

Take large oysters, wipe dry; fold a very thin slice of bacon around each and fix together with a toothpick; fry till bacon is crisp. Serve on hot pieces of toast without removing pins. [8]

FRONTISPIECE APPETIZERS CONTEMPORARY SOURCES

TARTE D'ALSACE (ALSATIAN TART)
Joan Toner, The Birchwood Inn, Lenox

Comment: "I'm delighted to share two recipes that our guests feel are special."

Bake a pie crust (to serve six) for 15 minutes at 400°.

2 cups onions, sliced
1 cup sour cream
3 eggs, beaten

2 tablespoons butter
Diced bacon
Salt and pepper

Saute onions in butter until dark brown. Mix sour cream, eggs, salt, pepper, and onions. Place in the pie crust, sprinkle with diced bacon. Bake 30 minutes at 400°.

HUEVOS ALBUQUERQUE
Joan Toner, The Birchwood Inn, Lenox

¾ to 1 lb. grated Monterey Jack cheese
24 oz. cottage cheese
½ teaspoon salt.
¼ teaspoon cayenne pepper
6 eggs, beaten

¼ cup melted butter or margarine
1 cup milk
1 cup Bisquick
½ cup canned green chilies, diced Bacos

Mix cheeses, salt, pepper, eggs, butter, milk and Bisquick and pour into a greased 9 x 13 pan. Add green chilies and press into mixture; do not stir. Top with Bacos. Bake at 350° for 50 minutes.

GRILLED SHIITAKE MUSHROOM ©
Jennifer Trainer
Author of "The Yachting Cookbook," with Liz Wheeler

Comment: With fresh shiitake mushrooms grown right in the Berkshires, I like to serve grilled shiitakes year-round as a tasty hors d'oeuvres or as a delicious side dish to meat.

One pound fresh shiitake mushroom caps, stems removed.

Marinade: 1 teaspoon minced ginger
1 teaspoon minced garlic
1 teaspoon sugar

3 tablespoons soy sauce
2 tablespoons sherry
4 tablespoons peanut oil

In a bowl, mix the marinade and toss with the shiitakes. Allow shiitakes to marinate for at least 15 minutes, and up to an hour. Light the grill, and when the coals are very hot, grill shiitakes 1 to 3 minutes on each side.

Remove from heat. If serving as an hors d'oeuvres, quarter the shiitakes and serve on a platter with toothpicks. If presenting as a side dish, serve the caps whole.

NOTE: Delftree shiitake mushrooms are grown year-round in a 19th century mill in North Adams. You can visit the Delftree farm stand at 234 Union Street and buy fresh shiitakes at a discount, or they can be shipped via UPS—even as far as Japan! Refrigerated, these mushrooms will stay fresh for up to three weeks. The phone number for Delftree Corporation is 413-664-4907.

QUESADILLA©
Jennifer Trainer, Williamstown/North Adams
Author of "The Yachting Cookbook" with Liz Wheeler

Comment: "On summer nights, I like to serve easy but elegant hors d'oeuvres that allow me to be outdoors with guests—not in the kitchen. Quesadillas are one of my favorites—not only do they take about ten minutes to make, but they can be cooked right on the grill (no pans to wash!) during cocktails. The following recipe was developed with my good friend and co-author Liz Wheeler."

Serves 2.

2 Large wheat tortillas
Monterey Jack or mild Cheddar cheese, shredded
Dried oregano
Scallions, thinly sliced
Jalapeneo peppers, thinly sliced
Vegetable oil

Light the grill. When grill is hot, place a tortilla flat on the grill, and scatter a handful of cheese on top of the tortilla to within 1 inch of the edge. Working quickly, sprinkle with a little oregano, a few scallions, and a few slivers of jalapenos. Scatter a thin layer of cheese on top (to provide the "glue") and cover with the other tortilla.

Cook for about 2 minutes or until the cheese begins to melt and a grill pattern appears on the tortilla. Flip the quesadilla carefully with a spatula and fry the other side until the cheese is melted, about 3 minutes.

Slide the quesadilla onto a cutting board and cut into wedges. Serve with guacamole, sour cream, and/or salsa.

Note: Quesadillas are also delicious served as a late afternoon snack, or for lunch. [20]

HOT WALNUT BEEF SPREAD
Susan Aceto

Comment:"This recipe, given me by a friend, won first prize in the hors d'ouvres and appetizer category in the 1977 yearly Plattsburgh (NY) Press Republican Recipe Contest. And, much to the embarrassment of my boys, it was entitled "Dried Beef Dip." Consequently, I have renamed the recipe.[11]

Mix until smooth:
8 oz. softened cream cheese
½ cup sour cream
2 tablespoons milk

Add:
2-½ oz. dried beef, cut fine*
2 tablespoons chopped green pepper
2 tablespoons minced onion

½ teaspoon pepper
¼ cup chopped walnuts

Heat in oven or microwave and spoon into small chafing dish to serve warm with crackers.

Dried beef is found in jars in the canned meat section of markets.

HOMEMADE BOURSIN CHEESE (Appetizer)
Audrey Sweeney

1   8 oz. cream cheese, softened
¼ teaspoon garlic powder
¾ teaspoon Fines Herbs
1 teaspoon parsley flakes

Mix together and let stand several hours. Serve with crackers.

DEVILED EGGS
Audrey Sweeney

Two dozen medium-sized eggs, hard-boiled and cooled.
Peel eggs and cut in half (long way)

Mix yolks with:
Two 4-½ oz. cans Deviled Ham
Mayonnaise to moisten
3 or 4 teaspoons sweet relish (green)

Fill halves of egg whites with yolk mixture, mounding. Arrange on large plate. Sprinkle with Paprika.

EGGPLANT APPETIZER
Dorothy Rowe

Good on pita bread or crackers.

4 cups peeled, cubed eggplant
½ cup chopped onion
4 cloves garlic, minced
2 stalks celery, sliced

3 tablespoons olive oil
½ cup black olives, chopped
2 teaspoons brown sugar
2 tablespoons white vinegar

Salt eggplant heavily and set aside for 15 minutes. Rinse salt off eggplant under running water while squeezing out bitter juices. Steam eggplant until tender. Sauté onion, garlic, and celery in olive oil until soft. Mix in eggplant, olives, capers, brown sugar, and vinegar and heat until warm. Eat hot, at room temperature, or chilled. Serves 10 as an appetizer.

VIENNA SAUSAGE APPETIZERS
Audrey Sweeney

Vienna sausages, cocktail wieners, or frankfurters
2 T. prepared horseradish
¼ cup currant jelly

Cut into bite-sized pieces. Heat together in saucepan about 10 minutes, stirring occasionally. Serve on toothpicks, with crackers.

HIDDEN VALLEY RANCH OYSTER CRACKERS
Dan Lee

"This is not my original recipe, but they are still absolutely delicious. Warning: They may become addicting."

12 - 16 oz. plain oyster crackers
1 package Hidden Valley Ranch Buttermilk Recipe Original Ranch Salad Dressing Mix
¼ teaspoon lemon pepper (optional)
½ - 1 teaspoon dill weed
¼ teaspoon garlic powder
¾ - 1 cup salad oil.

Combine salad dressing mix and oil; add dill weed, garlic powder and lemon pepper. Pour over crackers, stir to coat. Spread onto an ungreased cookie sheet and place in a warm oven for 15-20 minutes.

TITLE PAGE SOUPS OLD SOURCES

GENERAL DIRECTIONS FOR MAKING SOUP

Lean, Juicy Beef, Mutton, and Veal, form the basis of all good soups; therefore, it is advisable to procure those pieces which afford the richest succulence, and such as are fresh-killed. Stale meat renders them bad, and fat is not so well adapted for making them. The principal art in composing good rich soup, is so to proportion the several ingredients that the flavorful of one shall not predominate over another; and that all the articles of which it is composed, shall form an agreeable whole. To accomplish this, care must be taken that the roots and herbs are perfectly well cleaned and that the water is proportional to the quantity of meat and other ingredients. Generally a quart of water may be allowed to a pound of meat for soups, and half the quantity for gravies. In making soups or gravies, gentle stewing or simmering is incomparably the best. It may be remarked, however, that a really good soup can never be made but in a well-closed vessel, although, perhaps, greater wholesomeness is obtained by an occasional exposure to the air. Soups will, in general, take from three to six hours doing, and are much better prepared the day before they are wanted. When the soup is cold, the fat may be much more easily and completely removed; and when it is poured off, care must be taken not to disturb the settlings at the bottom of the vessel, which are so fine that they will escape through a sieve. [1]

However, a warm savory steam from the kitchen served to belie the apparently cheerless prospect before us. But when that smoking chowder came in, the mystery was delightfully explained. Oh, sweet friends! harken to me. It was made of small juicy clams, scarcely bigger than hazel nuts, mixed with pounded ship biscuit, and salted pork cut up into little flakes; the whole enriched with butter, and plentifully seasoned with pepper and salt.

Chowder for breakfast, and chowder for dinner and chowder for supper, till you began to look for fish-bones coming through your clothes.

HERMAN MELVILLE, *MOBY-DICK*

CHOWDER

General Rule for Soups. - One pint of fresh vegetables (one can), one pint of boiling water, one pint hot milk, one tablespoonful butter, one tablespoonful flour, salt and pepper. Cut the vegetables into bits and cook twenty minutes, or if you use canned vegetables, cook ten minutes. While it is cooking make the milk, butter and flour into white sauce, viz:-melt the butter, rub in the flour, add the hot milk and salt, and stir and cook until smooth. Then press as much as possible of the vegetables and water through a wire sieve and stir into white sauce and strain again. When you wish it very nice pour the hot soup over a cup of whipped cream and it will be foamy. [8]

CHOWDER

Fry slices of pork, cut very thin, in the dinner pot, hung high so they will not burn. Then put in a layer of fish cut small, a layer of onions, and then of potatoes, sliced as thin as a four pence; then fish, onions and potatoes again, till all are in, putting salt and pepper on each layer of onions. Cover with water and boil until potatoes are done. Put split crackers on top, and add a cup of milk five minutes before you take it up. [1]

CORN CHOWDER

1 quart raw sweet corn	1 pint sliced tomatoes
1 saltspoonful white pepper	1 onion
1 pint sliced potatoes	1 pint milk
1 large tablespoons butter	1 teaspoonful salt
A 2-inch cube fat salt pork	6 crisped crackers

Scrape the raw corn from the cob. Boil the cobs twenty minutes in water enough to cover them, then skim them out. Pare, soak, and scald the potatoes. Fry the onion in the salt pork fat, and strain the fat into the kettle with the corn water. Add the potatoes, corn, salt, and pepper. Simmer fifteen minutes, or till the potatoes and corn are tender. Add the butter and milk, and serve very hot with crisped crackers. [6]

OYSTER SOUP

One quart milk, one quart oysters, one pint cold water, one-quarter pound butter, four teaspoons flour, salt and pepper to taste. Put milk on to boil in double kettle, add the butter, pepper, salt and thickening, put the pint of cold water with the oysters and when they boil, skim and turn into the double kettle and serve. [2]

MULLIGATAWNY SOUP

Bones left from dinner, either turkey, chicken, veal or lamb. Four quarts of water, four stalks of celery, four tablespoons of butter, four tablespoons of flour, two onions, and two slices of carrot, salt and pepper, and one-half cup butter, then skim into the soup; in the butter remaining in the pan put flour and when that is brown, add bits of meat, whatever it may be, add the barley that has been simmering two hours. [2]

SCOTCH BROTH

Boil two pounds of mutton in two quarts of water, let it cool and skim. (The scraggy part of the neck will do.) Then put into the soup pot with one large slice of turnip, two of carrot, one onion and a stalk of celery, all cut fine, one-half cup barley. Simmer gently two hours. Stir together one tablespoon of flour and one of butter until smooth and mix with the soup. Salt and pepper to taste. [2]

Consomme or bouillon with a spoonful of grated cheese stirred in while soup is hot, is delicious and also nutritious. [4]

For Sickness At the Stomach.
Drink Spearmint tea and it will soon check it. [9]

A Good Quantity of old cheese is the best thing to eat when distressed by eating too much fruit or oppressed with any kind of food. [9]

BLACK BEAN SOUP

Ingredients:
One quart black beans
Two quarts cold water
One small onion
Two teaspoonfuls salt
One-half salt spoonful cayenne
One spoonful salt-mustard
One tablespoonful flour
Two tablespoons butter
One lemon
Two hard boiled eggs.

Mode: Soak the beans over night. In the morning pour off water and put them to boil in two quarts of cold water. Slice the onion and fry in one tablespoonful of butter; put with the beans, add a little celery, simmer until the beans are soft; add cold water to check the boiling and soften the beans; leaving about two quarts when done. Rub beans through strainer; add salt, pepper and mustard. When boiling thicken it with flour and butter, which have been mixed together. Season, cut the lemon and eggs into thin slices, put in tureen and pour the hot soup on them. Serve with croutons. [8]

SPLIT PEA SOUP

Soak one quart of split peas in lukewarm water for three hours. Pour off the water and boil the peas in three and a half quarts of salted water till they are thoroughly soft. Rub through a colander, and throw away whatever does not pass through. This will keep several days.

Take out the quantity needed for dinner (allowing a generous quart to three persons); boil in it a small piece of pork, onion, and a little white pepper and salt; strain and serve very hot, with small cubes of fried bread dropped into the tureen. [16]

SOUP WITHOUT WATER

Cut one pound of very lean beef, top or under round, into very small pieces, put them into a large jar, one that will hold nearly a gallon, filled up with every vegetable in the market, even a little lettuce, add salt and pepper, cover the jar closely, place it in a saucepan containing boiling water, or put in the oven of moderate temperature, cook for six hours. This will make sufficient for five persons. [15]

TOMATO SOUP

One quart tomatoes, one onion, two ounces flour, four ounces butter, two tablespoons sugar, one-half teaspoonful cayenne pepper, salt, three pints water, one pint milk. Boil tomatoes and onion in water three-quarters of an hour; add salt, pepper, sugar, butter and flour; rub smoothly together like thin cream; boil ten minutes. When both are boiling pour the milk into the tomatoes to prevent curdling. Serve with squares of toast. [8]

For Humors in the Blood.

Make a paste of sulphur, cream of tartar and molasses. Take a teaspoonful three mornings, skip three, take three. [1]

For Deafness. Take a strong glass bottle, nearly fill it with clarified honey. Insert the bottle into the center of an unbaked loaf of bread and bake thoroughly. Pour a little of the honey into your ears and protect them from air with cotton. [1]

TITLE PAGE SOUPS CONTEMPORARY SOURCES

"MANIAC'S" CLAM CHOWDER©
Jennifer Trainer

"The best way to make it is with clams you have dug yourself after dropping anchor in a secluded bay, but it is awfully good with fresh clams purchased at a local marina, too."

4 dozen hard-shell clams, scrubbed, or 1 quart shucked cooked clams with their broth
¼ pound cubed salt pork or 6 slices bacon
1 onion, coarsely chopped
6 medium potatoes, peeled and cut into ½" cubes
2 cups milk

2 cups half and half or evaporated milk
¾ stick unsalted butter (3 ounces)
salt
freshly ground pepper

Put the clams in a large pot with 1 cup water. Cover, bring to a boil, and cook until the shells open (about 10 minutes). Allow to cool and then shuck the clams and set aside. Pour off and reserve the broth, taking care not to disturb any sediment in the bottom of the pan.

Cook the salt pork in a large saucepan over medium heat until the fat runs. Add the onion and cook, stirring, until tender. Pour off half the fat.

Add the potatoes to the pan and stir well. Add the clam broth and enough water just to cover the potatoes. Simmer until these potatoes are tender.

Add the milk and half and half and bring to a simmer. Add the clams and butter and simmer for a few minutes until the clams are heated through and the butter is melted. (Do not boil or the clams will be tough.) Season with salt and pepper. Serves 4 to 6.[20]

CUCUMBER AND YOGURT SOUP©
Jennifer Trainer

According to Jennifer, this soup is better than air-conditioning.

3 or 4 cucumbers, peeled, halved, and seeded	1 teaspoon salt	Tabasco or cayenne (ground red) pepper
2 tablespoons cider or rice wine vinegar	2 cups plain yogurt	2 teaspoons dried dill or 2 tablespoons fresh dill leaves
1 tablespoon sugar	1 cup ice water	2 to 3 scallions, finely sliced

Grate the cucumbers coarsely into a bowl. Stir in the vinegar, sugar and salt. Allow the cucumber to marinate for fifteen minutes. Drain the mixture through a sieve, pressing firmly to remove the excess liquid.

Combine the cucumbers with the yogurt. Slowly stir in enough ice water to make a thick, creamy soup. Season to taste with salt and Tabasco. Stir in the dill and sprinkle the soup with scallions. Serve cold. Serves 4 to 6.[20]

KALE SOUP
Wendyll Wells Champoux

4 large potatoes	1 medium onion, chopped
2-½ quarts water	¼ cup olive oil
¾ to 1 lb. linguica*	salt & pepper
1 lb. kale	chicken stock

*Linguica is a garlicky Portuguese sausage easily found in most large markets. You may use chorizo instead but your soup will be very spicy!

Peel and dice potatoes and place in covered pot containing 2-½ quarts boiling water. Slice linguica into slim coins and saute in heavy skillet until lightly browned. Once browned, turn heat down, cover and wait for potatoes to soften. Mash softened potatoes in the water, add linguica to water and chicken stock to the empty skillet to gather the sausage drippings and add to soup along with chopped onion.

Let soup simmer for approximately 10 minutes. Meanwhile, wash kale, remove the thick middle ribs with a knife and bundle kale so that you can chop it into long, thin ribbons. Add the kale to soup with olive oil and salt and pepper to taste. It's best served about 5 minutes after kale has been added so that it's bright green and crisp

COLD BUTTER MILK SOUP
Jytte Brooks

Old fashioned Danish summer soup, which is still popular today.

2 quarts butter milk
1 cup milk
6 egg yolks

8 Tablespoons sugar
1 lemon
1 teaspoon vanilla extract

In a food mixer cream egg yolks and sugar until fine. Add milk and make a custard in a double boiler. Slowly add butter milk and vanilla. Mix well and refrigerate for several hours. Serve with thin slices of lemon and croutons in the soup.

RUSSIAN MEAT AND LENTIL SOUP
Vivian Tampashan

1 lb. lean lamb
Cumin
8 cups water
Tomatoes
Salt and pepper to taste

Parsley
1 cup dried lentils
Coriander
2 tablespoons butter
2 potatoes, peeled and cubed

Soup Topping:
½ cup dried apricots
2 finely minced garlic cloves
½ cup dried prunes
cloves
⅓ cup chopped walnuts
1 cup Yogurt
lime wedges

Combine in a big pot: lamb, water, salt and pepper. Cover and simmer one hour, skimming off foam. Stir the lentils into this mixture, and cook 15 minutes. Meanwhile, in a heavy skillet heat the butter, and saute the potatoes, browning evenly. Then add the potatoes, apricots, prunes and walnuts to the main pot and simmer 30 minutes. Add more water if necessary.

Cumin, tomatoes, parsley and coriander, in the amount desired, may be stirred into the soup before serving.

For the soup topping, which should stand at least an hour, mix the garlic and yogurt. Place a dollop of this atop each serving, and place lemon wedges on the side. The number served varies, depending on whether this is used as a main dish or first course. Low fat dish.

PUMPKIN AND CIDER SOUP
Clifford Rudisill - Village Inn

Ingredients:
1 medium pumpkin
1 gallon apple cider
2 teaspoons ground cinnamon
2 teaspoons salt
1 teaspoon ground ginger
1 teaspoon ground cloves
1 teaspoon nutmeg

Method: Cut and quarter 1 medium pumpkin. Peel skin and remove seeds. Cut quarters into large, diced pieces of pumpkin. Place in sauce pot with seasonings and 1 quart of the apple cider. Bring to a boil, cover and reduce to a simmer. Cook until pumpkin pieces are tender. Puree in a food blender. Return to sauce pot, add remaining cider, bring to a boil, reduce to a simmer. Cook for 30 minutes. Makes 1-½ gallons.

VELVET ZUCCHINI SOUP
Ted Giddings

2 medium zucchini
2 tablespoons margarine
1 clove garlic, minced
½ teaspoon curry powder
1 can chicken broth or 2 envelopes with water
½ cup light cream or a small can Carnation evaporated milk

Slice zucchini and saute with onion and garlic in margarine for 5 minutes. Add curry powder and simmer covered for 15 minutes. Place in blender. Add cream and broth and blend again.

CHICKEN SOUP DELUXE
Oralie Thurston

1 whole broiler-fryer chicken
3 cups cold water
1 bay leaf
1-½ teaspoon salt
½ cup chopped cabbage
1 teaspoon chopped parsley
½ teaspoon tarragon leaves
½ teaspoon basil leaves

1 t. chopped celery leaves
½ teaspoon pepper
¾ cup chopped green onions, tops included
½ cup chopped celery
¾ cup chopped green pepper
1 can (16 oz.) tomatoes
1 T. vinegar

In large pan place chicken with cold water, salt, parsley, tarragon, basil, celery leaves and pepper. Cook for about one hour or until chicken falls readily from bones. Pour off broth and refrigerate to separate from fat. When chicken is cool, remove bones and skin and chop chicken into bite-size pieces. Skim fat from refrigerated broth and melt the fat in a soup kettle over medium heat. Saute onions, celery, and green pepper for five minutes. Add tomatoes (cut up), vinegar, bay leaf, broth and chopped cabbage. Simmer over low heat for ten to fifteen minutes. Add cooked chicken and heat just to serving temperature.

Makes four to six generous servings.

ZUCCHINI MINESTRONE
Edith Taskin

3 tablespoons oil
1-½ c. chopped onions
1-½ c. thinly sliced celery
1 cup diced carrots
½ cup diced green peppers
4 cups zucchini, cubed
4 cups tomatoes, peeled and chopped
6 cups water
Salt, garlic powder, onion powder, and black pepper

In large pot heat oil, add onions, celery, carrots and peppers and saute until onions are tender. Add zucchini, tomatoes, water and spices. Cover and simmer 45 minutes.

Add:
½ cup uncooked elbow macaroni
1 can (20 oz.) red kidney beans, undrained
2 teaspoon basil leaves
½ teaspoon oregano

Simmer covered, 15 minutes. Garnish with parsley and Parmesan cheese.

HAMBURG SOUP
Audrey Sweeney

1-½ lbs. hamburg
1 medium onion, chopped fine
1 28 oz. can tomatoes
4 cups water

3 cans consomme
1 can tomato soup
1 soup can tomato juice

4 carrots, chopped fine
1 bay leaf
3 stalks celery, chopped fine

Salt and pepper to taste
1 T. sugar
8 T. barley

Brown meat and onions, drain well. Put all ingredients in large pot. Simmer covered at least two hours or all day. Serves 10. (Makes 18 soup ladles-full. Freezes well.)

FOREWORD   EGGS CHEESE PASTA RICE BEANS OLD SOURCES

As she stooped above the chafing dish . . . she bent to break the eggs into the dish . . . ."Look! Fresh mushrooms!" She cried, uncovering another dish and as the warm savour of the cooking filled the air. She scooped the smoking mess of eggs and mushrooms into their two plates.

EDITH WHARTON, *THE GODS ARRIVE*

In the dell of Shadow Brook, Eustace Bright and his little friends had eaten their dinner. They had brought plenty of good things from Tanglewood, in their baskets, and had spread them out on the stumps of trees, and on mossy trunks, and had feasted merrily, and made a very nice dinner indeed. After it was over, nobody felt like stirring.

NATHANIEL HAWTHORNE,
THE WONDERBOOK FOR GIRLS AND BOYS

FONDUE

Brillat-Savarin

Savarin gives this receipt, which he says is taken from the papers of a Swiss bailiff. He says: "It is a dish of Swiss origin, is healthy, savory, appetizing, quickly made, and, moreover is always ready to present to unexpected guests."

He relates an anecdote of the sixteenth century of a M. de Madot, newly appointed Bishop of Belley, who at a feast given in honor of his arrival, mistaking the fondue for cream, ate it with a spoon instead of a fork. This caused so much comment that the next day no two people met who did not say: "Do you know how the new bishop ate his fondue last night?" "Yes, he ate it with a spoon. I have it from an eye-witness." And soon the news spread over the diocese. [16]

RECEIPT

"Weigh as many eggs as you have guests. Take one third their weight of Gruyere cheese, and one sixth their weight of butter. Beat the eggs well in a saucepan; add the cheese, grated, and the butter. Put the saucepan on the fire and stir until the mixture is soft and creamy; then add salt, more or less, according to the age of the cheese, and a generous amount of pepper, which is one of the positive characters of the dish. Serve on a hot plate. Bring in the best wine, drink roundly of it, and you will see wonders." [16]

SCOTCH WOODCOCK

One tablespoonful each flour and butter rubbed together, six or seven hard boiled eggs chopped fine, one pint milk, one small teaspoonful anchovy paste, a little mustard. Serve on small squares of buttered toast. [8]

DUMPLINGS WITH BAKING POWDER

2 cupfuls of flour
½ teaspoonful of salt
2 teaspoonfuls of baking powder
1 cupful of milk

Mix the flour, salt, and baking powder well together, then stir in quickly the milk. Have the dough quite soft. Drop the batter from a spoon into the stew, or into boiling water; or, if preferred, make the dough just consistent enough to roll, and cut it into squares. The stew must not be allowed to stop simmering after the dumplings are in; and they must be served immediately after being taken from the pot, or they will fall. It will take ten minutes to cook them. [16]

DUMPLINGS WITH SUET

1 cupful of chopped suet
2 scant cupfuls of flour
1 teaspoonful of salt
½ cupful of cold water

Mix together lightly the flour, suet and salt; then with a knife stir in quickly the water. The dough must be soft, but not sticky. Put it on a board and roll it lightly to one inch thickness, and place it on the boiling stew in one cake. The stew must not stop boiling for a moment or the dumpling will fall. Cook for one hour. The dough may be rolled into balls if preferred. When the dumpling is put in, draw the pot forward where it will heat quickly, and not arrest the boiling. When it is thoroughly hot, place it where it will simmer continually during the hour of cooking. If this rule is observed, it will be light and spongy. Where cooked meat is used, which does not require such long cooking, the dumplings may be boiled in water. [16]

To Keep Butter. To have sweet butter in dog days and through the vegetable seasons, send stone pots to honest, neat dairy people, and procure it packed down in May, and let them be brought in in the night or cool rainy mornings, and partake of no heat from the horse, and set the pots in the coldest part of your cellar.[1]

RICE CRUSTS
Miss Ward

Cook one cup of cold boiled rice in the double boiler in milk enough to make a thin mixture, and until the rice is very soft. Add one tablespoonful of sugar, a little salt, one egg, and flour enough to make it hold together. Spread on the pan, having the mixture one third of an inch thick. Bake in a hot oven. Split and eat with syrup. [6]

PORK AND BEANS — New Hampshire

Soak a pint of small white beans over night. In the morning pour off the water, pour on a pint of cold water, and set at the back of the range to simmer slowly for three quarters of an hour.

Place the beans in a bean pot with half a pound of scored salt pork in the middle, half a teaspoonful of dry mustard, salt, white pepper, and a half pint of white sugar. Add water from time to time, as it grows dry, and bake twelve hours. [16]

CHEESE FLUFF
Mrs. Edwin E. Cooney

3 eggs
6 slices bread
1½ cups milk
¼ lb. cheese, or more

Remove crusts from bread, cut in half and place in greased casserole. On each slice of bread, put a slice of cheese, also butter and salt. Beat eggs and milk and pour over bread. Let stand about ½ hour or longer. Bake 40 minutes in 350° oven. Serve at once. [13]

YORKSHIRE PUDDING

Put two cupfuls of flour into a bowl, and mix in one half a teaspoonful of salt. Beat up three eggs, and stir them into the flour; then add two cupfuls of milk. Stir until the mixture is smooth, then turn it into a pan containing a little of the drippings from the roast beef. Let the batter be only one inch deep in the pan. Bake thirty to forty minutes. Cut the pudding in squares, and place it around the roast beef. [16]

RICE À LA RISTORI

Wash well and drain a quarter of a pound of good Italian rice; shred two ounces of bacon into small pieces, and place them in a saucepan with a medium-sized, chopped-up, raw cabbage, letting them steam for thirty minutes. Add a pinch of salt, half a pinch of pepper, and a teaspoonful of chopped parsley; put in the rice, and moisten with half a pint of white broth. Cook for fully a quarter of an hour longer, and serve with grated Parmesan cheese sprinkled over it. [4]

To Preserve Eggs. One pint of coarse salt, one pint of unslaked lime, to a pail of water. Eggs will keep sound and wholesome for years in this, if kept in a cool place. [1]

A pinch of powdered sugar and another of cornstarch beaten in with the yolks of eggs will keep an omelet from collapsing. [3]

MACARONI WITH CHEESE
Mrs. E. P. Carpenter

Take one-fourth of a package of macaroni, break into a dish, set on the back of the stove and let heat gradually, covering at first with cold water; when it comes to a boil cook until tender; drain off the water; butter the baking dish; put in a thick layer of macaroni, then a thin layer of grated cheese with pieces of butter, and a thin covering of cream, adding pepper and salt; repeat this until the dish is filled, having cheese for last layer; moisten the whole with sweet milk and bake. [8]

CREAMED EGGS

Boil twelve eggs hard and slice them in thin rings; put in a baking dish first a layer of bread crumbs, then a layer of egg, then a layer of crumbs, and so on until the dish is filled; season with salt, pepper and butter, then pour a cup of sweet cream over all and bake to a nice brown in a moderately-heated oven.
Jennie Walther, 203 East Eighth Street, St. Paul, Minn. [8]

MOCK EGGS
Mrs. J. T. McCleary - Mankato, Minn.

Prepare a white corn starch pudding, mold in eggshells, after carefully removing all of the egg. Serve in colored ice glasses, with cream. [8]

RISOTTO À LA MILANESE

Chop rather fine one good-sized, very sound, peeled onion. Melt two ounces of very good butter in a saucepan on a very brisk fire; add the onions, brown them for six or seven minutes, or until they have obtained a good golden color; then add ten ounces of well-picked Italian rice (a heaped cupful), then two good-sized chopped truffles; stir well with the spatula without ceasing for one and a half minutes. Then add one quart of boiling and strained white broth, lightly stir once only, and cook for fourteen minutes. Add six fine chopped mushrooms, and little by little, at intervals, another quart of boiling white broth—stirring almost constantly with the wooden spatula while cooking, very rapidly, for ten minutes more. Season with a heavy half-teaspoonful of salt, a light saltspoonful of white pepper, adding one and a half ounces of grated Swiss cheese, and a heaped tea-spoonful of Spanish branch saffron, diluted in two tablespoons of hot white broth, and strained. Cook for three or four minutes longer, stirring continually meanwhile; then pour it into a hot soup-tureen, and send to the table with a little grated Swiss cheese, separate. A little beef-marrow can be added to advantage, by making a small cavity in the centre, while yet in the pan, one minute before the time to serve, and plunging into it one table-spoonful of marrow. [4]

To break up a Fresh Cold. Nothing is better than a glass of hot Flip on going to bed. Put the poker in the fire to heat. Mix some ginger and molasses in a beer mug. Pour on some sour cider. Plunge in the red hot poker and stir it up till it foams well. This is a very agreeable cure. Warm the bed hot with the warmingpan and put in some hot bricks. A fine sweat will carry off the cold. [1]

POACHED EGGS

Boil in a deep saucepan three quarters of water with a heavy pinch of salt and three drops of vinegar. Have easily at hand twelve fresh eggs. When, and only when, the water boils, rapidly but carefully crack six of them, one by one. As success to have them in proper shape and cooked to perfection depends upon how they are handled, special care should be taken to crack them as rapidly as possible, carefully avoiding to break the yolks, and dropping each one right on the spot where the water bubbles, and as near the boiling point as possible. Poach for one minute and a quarter from the time that the water boils after the eggs were put in. Lift them up with a skimmer, lay them on the freshly prepared toasts, or use for any other desired purpose; and repeat the same with the other six. If handled strictly as above described you will have them to perfection, and no necessity of trimming any superfluous adherings; serve when required.[4]

SCRAMBLED EGGS

Melt three ounces of butter in a saucepan, break into it twelve fresh eggs; season with a pinch of salt, half a pinch of pepper, and a third of a pinch of grated nutmeg. Mix thoroughly without stopping for three minutes, using a spatula, and having the pan on a very hot stove. Turn into a warm tureen, add a little verjuice or lemon juice, and send to the table very hot. [4]

FOREWORD EGGS CHEESE PASTA RICE BEANS CONTEMPORARY SOURCES

FUSILLI WITH PEANUT SAUCE

Jennifer Trainer
Great New England Cooks ©

A filling pasta salad tastes great with a pork salad. This can be prepared ahead of time and kept at cool room temperature. Using the boiling water from the pasta to smooth out the peanut sauce saves water and time—both precious commodities.

½ pound fusilli or corkscrew pasta
1 tablespoons sesame oil
sesame seeds

Peanut sauce:
4 to 5 tablespoons peanut butter (see note)
2 teaspoons brown or granulated sugar
2 cloves garlic, finely chopped
2 teaspoons finely chopped fresh gingerroot
2 tablespoons vegetable oil
2 tablespoons soy sauce
1 tablespoons cider vinegar
4 to 5 tablespoons boiling water (from cooking pasta)

Bring a large saucepan of salted water to a boil. Cook the fusilli until just tender (about ten minutes).

While the pasta cooks, combine all the sauce ingredients except the water in a small mixing bowl. With a whisk, slowly blend the liquid ingredients with the peanut butter, making a stiff paste. Whisk in the hot water by the tablespoonful until the sauce has the consistency of heavy cream.

Drain the fusilli, shaking off the excess water. Add the noodles to the sauce, sprinkle with the sesame oil, and toss. Sprinkle sesame seeds over the top. Serve within 4 hours. Do not refrigerate or the noodles will become stiff and sticky. Serves 3 to 4.

Note: If using commercially processed peanut butter, omit the sugar from the sauce; add it later, if necessary, after tasting.

ELDER SERVICES OF BERKSHIRE COUNTY CONTEST 1ST
STATE CONTEST 2ND

PASTA & BEANS (FAGIOLI) WITH VEGGIES
Maria Celia Rash

INGREDIENTS:
3 tablespoons Safflower oil or olive oil
2 teaspoons of Mrs. Dash
1 large green pepper
2 stalks celery
1 large onion
2 cloves garlic - minced
2 large fresh tomatoes

1 20-oz. can white or red kidney beans
Parmesan cheese (optional)
3 cups water
½ lb. pasta (linguine or noodles)
2½ quarts water
Parsley and cherry tomatoes (garnish)

INSTRUCTIONS: Heat oil in iron skillet or electric pan and stir fry green pepper and celery on medium heat until tender; add onion and garlic, stirring until cooked. Add tomatoes, cook 15 to 20 minutes. Add 2 teaspoons of Mrs. Dash. Add 3 cups water and let vegetables sauce boil on low heat for 3 minutes. LAST—Put in thoroughly drained beans. Stir lightly and set aside on simmer.

In separate pan, bring 2½ quarts of water to a boil. Put in pasta and cook for 10 to 12 minutes (7 or 8 minutes for noodles). Drain and add to the beans and vegetable sauce—Garnish with parsley and cherry tomatoes.

Serve with Parmesan cheese, if desired. Number of servings 4 or 5.

NOODLE PUDDING
Roselle Chartock

As the Berkshires are like so many parts of America, a "tossed salad" of ethnic groups, this recipe reflects my heritage, Polish-Jewish, although many groups have similar dishes, we all know what's good.

½ lb. broad noodles, cooked and drained.
1 cup sour cream
1 cup cottage cheese
4 or more eggs - beaten

½ stick melted butter
½ cup chopped apple and/or raisins
½ cup sugar
Dash of salt, pepper, cinnamon

Mix together all ingredients. Pour into greased baking dish. Bake for one hour in 300° oven. Let stand for 10 minutes before cutting. Can also be enjoyed cold.

PASTA PRIMAVERA
Maria Celia Rash

1 lb. thin spaghetti
2 tablespoons olive oil
1 garlic clove, minced
1 teaspoon or 1 fresh sprig
½ teaspoon oregano
½ teaspoon of Mrs. Dash (original blend) yellow top
2 tablespoons butter or margarine

2 tablespoons grated Parmesan cheese
1 cup broccoli florets
¾ cup thin strips carrots
¾ cup each red and green pepper strips
1 cup shredded zucchini
salt and pepper to taste

While pasta is cooking (as directed on package), cook broccoli and carrots in 2 cups of boiling water for 2 minutes (remove and cool).

Saute pepper strips in oil until tender. Add zucchini and garlic; saute 1 minute. Add carrots, broccoli, pasta and seasonings. Last, add butter and toss to coat. Sprinkle with Parmesan cheese. Makes about 4 servings.

SICILIAN EGG TOAST
Linda-Marie Nuciforo

In past days, we kids walked home from Tucker School at noon for home cooked lunch. On meatless Fridays, we looked forward to our mother preparing one of our favorites: Sicilian Egg Toast.

Makes a nice light supper served with a mixed green salad.

4 slices thick Vienna bread
3 or 4 eggs
¼ cup milk
salt and pepper to taste

1 clove of minced garlic
1 tablespoons chopped parsley
⅓ cup grated Parmesan cheese

Lightly sprinkle bread slices with water and set aside. Beat eggs, add milk and other ingredients. Brush pan with olive oil. When oil is hot, fry bread which has been dipped into egg mixture (do not soak) until golden brown on both sides.

LENTIL-CHEESE LOAF
Joy Hayes

1 cup uncooked lentils
1 small onion
1 bay leaf
2 tablespoons melted butter or margarine

1 egg
1 small onion, grated
Progresso Seasoned breadcrumbs
½ pound grated cheddar cheese
1 to 2 teaspoon thyme
1 small can tomato sauce

Cover with water and cook lentils with small, halved onion and bay leaf until tender—45 to 60 minutes. Drain if necessary. Remove onion pieces and bay leaf.

Measure 2 cups cooked lentils into a bowl. Add egg, grated onion and thyme. Add bread crumbs until the mixture, when mixed, is moist but consistent.

Pat into a greased loaf pan and bake 30 to 35 minutes until top turns golden brown. Remove from oven, add tomato sauce. Let stand for a few minutes for sauce to be slightly warm. Good served with steamed, buttered carrots and a green salad.

WELSH RAREBIT
Clifford Rudisill

2 lbs. cheddar cheese, grated
2 tablespoons butter
16 oz. dark beer
2 eggs, slightly beaten

Worcestershire Sauce, to taste
Salt to taste
Red pepper to taste
Lemon juice to taste

In a double boiler, melt the butter. Stir in beer. When this mixture is hot, stir in grated cheese with a fork. When melted, add slightly beaten eggs. Adjust seasoning with Worcestershire sauce, salt, red pepper, and lemon juice.

Serve immediately over toast or hot biscuits. Yield: 16 servings

RICE CASSEROLE
William Swan

A good accompaniment to roast leg of lamb, roast beef, etc.

Rice, minute or regular, for six servings
1 small can 4 or 6 oz. Old El Paso or Ortega Green chilies
1 pint sour cream, regular or diet

Cook rice until done, drain and fluff. Take seeds out of chilies and cut into long, thin strips. Grease casserole dish and layer rice, chilies, and shredded Monterey Jack cheese in dish until all ingredients are used. Stir in the sour cream and mix well so that ingredients are evenly distributed. Bake, uncovered, at about 350° degrees until brown and bubbly, approximately 30 to 45 minutes.

PASTA WITH PISTACHIO LEMON PESTO
Keith Emerling

Serves 4 people as an appetizer.

3 oz. by weight of imported Parmesan Cheese, no rind
5 oz. by weight, all natural low salt Pistachios in shell
1 medium to large lemon washed
⅓ cup Walnut or Hazelnut Oil at room temperature
⅔ lb Plain fresh linguine

All ingredients should be fresh and of good quality.

Equipment:
Cheese grater with fine teeth
Measuring utensils
4 qt. sauce pot
Mixing utensils
Strainer
Warmed serving container

Preparation:
Finely grate Parmesan Cheese. Shell Pistachios, chop in a food processor or crush in a plastic bag until fine in texture. Zest lemon on grater, bright yellow part only. In a bowl mix these ingredients well. Can be prepared in advance up to this point.

To Serve:
Heat sauce pot filled two thirds with water, some salt and a touch of oil. Bring to a boil, add pasta and stir once. Cook for three minutes or until "al dente". Drain well. Return to empty pot and mix alternately with reserved ingredients and oil until pasta is thoroughly coated, use more oil if needed. Serve in a warm container.

FRIANDISES
Elizabeth B. Urmy

8 to 10 eggs
12 thin slices of ham
¼ to ½ pound Swiss cheese (American style) Butter
½ pint heavy cream (This is the original recipe! I use ½ plus ½ or milk!)

Beat eggs with a little cream. Salt and pepper. Heat a small round pan with a little butter in it. When butter is hot, fill a large kitchen spoon with ½ egg mixture and pour in pan—just enough for thin omelet. Cook on each side and put on plate; cover with slice of ham and roll it up. Continue until 12 are done. Then pack tightly into ovenproof dish. Grate lots and lots of cheese over them, cover completely. One half hour before serving, pour cream over them and place in moderate oven until cream starts baking. Then put under broiler to brown the cheese. This serves six. May be done ahead up to the point of adding cream or milk.

CASSEROLE OF WILD RICE
Carolyn E. Banfield

1 tablespoons butter/margarine, melted
½ cup chopped celery
3 tablespoons finely chopped onion
4 chicken bouillon cubes, dissolved in 1 quart boiling water
1 cup wild rice, washed
1 cup long-grain white rice
2 tablespoons soy sauce
½ teaspoon salt
1 tablespoons chopped parsley

Preheat oven to 350°. In hot butter in small skillet, saute celery and onion until tender, about five minutes. Combine with remaining ingredients, except parsley, in 2 quart covered casserole. Bake covered about forty minutes. Remove cover; bake 15 minutes. Garnish with parsley. Makes 6 to 8 servings.

EGG CAKES WITH TOMATO SAUCE
Anita M. Nuciforo

This dish was once served on Good Friday or other meatless days. It has since become a favorite "company's coming for dinner" dish.

Egg Cakes
4 large eggs
1 tablespoon olive oil
½ cup grated Romano or Parmesan cheese
⅓ cup dry bread crumbs
dash salt
¼ teaspoon black pepper
1 tablespoon parsley, minced
1 garlic clove, minced

Tomato Sauce
1 medium onion, diced
2 garlic cloves; whole
2 tablespoons olive oil
1 6 oz. can tomato paste
2½ cups water
1 tablespoon basil flakes
1 teaspoon oregano (if desired)
1 teaspoon sugar

Egg cakes:
Beat eggs and olive oil together with fork. To egg mixture, add next 6 ingredients, and mix well. Mixture will be loose.

Tomato Sauce:
Saute onion and garlic in ten inch frying pan. Do not burn garlic. Stir and dissolve tomato paste in water. Add all other seasonings. Simmer gently uncovered for approximately 35 minutes, or until sauce thickens. Stir occasionally. Discard garlic cloves.

To complete: Gently spoon about ⅓ cup of egg batter for each cake on top of hot sauce (not bubbling). Do not crowd as they will double in size. Cover immediately and simmer on low heat 20 minutes or until egg is firm.

To Serve: Scoop egg cakes from pan into soup bowls and spoon tomato sauce over them. Serves 3 or 4 (6-8 cakes).

PREFACE BREAD BREAKFAST OLD SOURCES

Do you really want to know "whether oatmeal is preferable to pie as an American national food"? I suppose the best answer I can give to your question is to tell you what is my own practice. Oatmeal in the morning, as an architect lays a bed of concrete to form a base for his superstructure. Pie when I can get it; that is, of the genuine sort, for I am not patriotic.

OLIVER WENDELL HOLMES,
OVER THE TEACUPS

Life, within doors, has few pleasance prospects than a neatly arranged and well-provisioned breakfast-table. We come to it freshly, in the dewy youth of the day, and when our spiritual and sensual elements are in better accord than at a later period; so that the material delights of the morning meal are capable of being fully enjoyed, without any very grievous reproaches, whether gastric or conscientious, for yielding even a trifle overmuch to the animal department of our nature.

NATHANIEL HAWTHORNE,
HOUSE OF SEVEN GABLES

POPCORN BREAD
Paul Metcalf - Herman Melville's Great-grandson

⅔ cup boiling water
⅔ cup cold milk
1 package dry yeast
⅙ cup sugar
3 cups popped popcorn, run through blender until crumbled
½ teaspoon salt
2 eggs
¼ cup melted butter
5 cups flour

Mix water and milk in a large bowl. Stir in yeast and sugar and let rest about 10 minutes until foamy. Stir in the popcorn and salt, then eggs and butter. Slowly blend in the flour. Knead on a floured surface for 10 minutes, until dough is no longer sticky and is easy to work with. Oil a large bowl and put the dough in it. Cover and let rise in a warm place ½ hour. Punch down, cover and let rise ½ hour again. Shape into loaves and let rise covered for one hour. Bake in greased pans (8½ x 4½ x 2½) for 40 minutes at 350°.

Optional: Brush with melted butter sprinkle with coarse salt.

BREAD

Bread when taken out of the oven is unprepared for the stomach. It should ripen before it is eaten. It goes through a Change similar to that in newly brewed beer. During this Change it sends off a large portion of carbon or unhealthy gas, and imbibes a large portion of Oxygen or healthy gas. Bread not only has one fifth more nitrogenize, according to the computation of physicians, after ripening, but imparts a much greater degree of cheerfulness. He that eats old ripe Bread will have a much greater flow of animal spirits than he would were he to eat unripe bread. It should always ripen where the air is pure, never in a cellar, or a close cupboard, nor in a bedroom. [1]

WAFFLES

2 cups flour (heaping measure after sifting)
½ teaspoon salt
2 teaspoons baking powder.

Sift together. Add to dry ingredients yolks of two eggs and 1 scant cup of milk, beating well so as to make a smooth batter. Stir in two tablespoons melted butter, and stiffly beaten whites of two eggs. [12]

JOHNNY CAKE

1 egg
½ cup brown sugar
1 tablespoons butter
1 tablespoons lard
1 cup sour milk
1 teaspoon soda

1 cup sweet milk
2 teaspoons baking powder
½ teaspoon salt
1 cup corn meal
1 cup white flour [12]

GRAHAM BREAD

1 cup graham flour
2 cups white flour
2 heaping teaspoons baking powder
1 level teaspoon salt

Sift above, look over husks and add ½ cup sugar, 1 egg (cream together); 1¼ cups sweet milk. Add nuts and raisins or nuts alone. Let rise 20 minutes and bake slowly 1 hour. [12]

MASHED POTATO ROLLS

1 cup hot mashed potato
2 eggs
½ cup butter

Cream butter and potato, add eggs and beat. One teaspoon salt, 1 tablespoon sugar—or more if liked rather sweet. One Fleischman's yeast cake dissolved in cup luke warm water. Set in warm place for about two hours. Then add flour, about 4 cups, let rise again. When light pat out thin and cut with biscuit cutter. Spread with melted butter, fold over and pinch together. Bake.[12]

BAKING DAY
How to Heat the Oven.

Some people consider it economical to heat Ovens with fagots, brush and light stuff. Hard wood heats it quicker and hotter. Take four foot wood split fine, and pile it criss-cross so as to nearly fill the oven, and keep putting in. A Roaring fire for an hour or more is usually enough. The top and sides will at first be covered with black soot. See that it is all burned off. Rake the coals over the bottom of the Oven and let them lie a minute. Then sweep it out clean. If you can hold your hand inside while you count Forty it is about right for flour bread; to count twenty is right for Rye and Indian. If it too hot, wet an old broom two or three times and turn it round near the top of the oven till it dries; this prevents pies and cake from scorching on top. When you go into a new house, heat your oven two or three times to get it seasoned, before you use it.[1]

SCONES

2 cups flour
1 teaspoon salt
3 teaspoons Royal Baking Powder
2 tablespoons sugar
2 tablespoons shortening
2 eggs
⅓ cup milk

Try them for luncheon or tea. Sift dry ingredients, add shortening and rub in very lightly. Beat eggs until light, add milk to eggs and then add slowly to the mixture. Roll out half an inch thick on a floured board. Cut into 3 inch squares and fold over, making them three cornered. Brush with milk, dust with sugar and bake for about 25 minutes in a hot oven.[12]

SCRAPPLE

Mrs. James Arthur Burbank

Take fresh pork and boil until tender. Remove all bones and put meat through meat chopper. Put meat back into the liquor. Season with salt and pepper. Stir in Indian meal to make a good thickening as you would for mush. Set away to cool, then slice and fry.[12]

A GROUP OF RECEIPTS FROM A NEW ENGLAND KITCHEN
(Supplied by Susan Coolidge)

Many of the receipts in this little "group" have never before appeared in print. They are copies from old grandmother and great-grandmother receipt books, tested by generations of use, and become, at this time, traditional in the families to which they belong. They are now given to the public as examples of the simple but dainty cooking of a by-gone day, which, while differing in many points from the methods of our own time, in its way is no less delicious. [16]

THIN INDIAN BREAD — VERMONT

Mix together two cupfuls of meal, a tablespoonful of lard, and a teaspoonful of salt; scald with boiling water. Thin it with a large cupful of cold milk and two well-beaten eggs. Spread thin on a large buttered pan, and bake till brown in an oven only moderately hot. [16]

BOSTON BROWN BREAD

One pint of yellow cornmeal, scalded with a small quantity of boiling water, just enough to wet it thoroughly. Let it stand ten minutes. Then add enough cold water to make a soft batter. Add one quarter pint of brewer's yeast, one quarter pint of molasses, one pint of rye meal, one half teaspoonful of salt, and one saltspoonful of soda. Beat it well together, and set it to rise over night. When light, stir it thoroughly, put it into a buttered tin, sprinkle a little flour over the top, and set it to rise again. Bake about two hours. It is excellent cut into slices and toasted. [16]

DABS — CONNECTICUT

A pint of cornmeal, thoroughly scalded with hot water. Rub into it a dessertspoonful of butter, two eggs beaten very light, a wineglassful of cream or milk, and a little salt. Butter a tin pan, and drop the mixture from a spoon upon it. Bake in a moderate oven. [16]

BREAKFAST ROLLS

6 ounces of butter
1 pint of warm water
1 tablespoon of salt
1 pint baker's yeast
Flour enough to make a stiff dough

Mix the night before. [9]

FRENCH PANCAKES (No Soda)
Miss Purloa

3 eggs
1 cup milk
½ teaspoonful salt

1 teaspoonful sugar
½ cup flour
½ tablespoonful salad oil

Beat the yolks and whites separately. Add the milk, sugar, and salt to the yolks. Pour one third of this mixture on the flour, and stir to a smooth paste. Add the remainder of the milk, and beat well; then add the oil. Heat and butter a small frying-pan, and pour into it enough of the mixture to cover the pan; when brown, turn and brown the other side. Spread with butter and sugar or jelly; roll up, and sprinkle with powdered sugar. [9]

STEAMED GRAHAM BREAD

3 cups graham flour
1 cup white flour
2 teaspoons soda
1 teaspoon salt
¾ cup molasses
2½ cups sour milk

To the dry ingredients mixed, add molasses and milk; turn into well greased mold, fill not more than ⅔ full. Two and a half cups of sweet milk and 4 teaspoons of baking powder may be used instead of sour milk and soda. Add cup of seeded raisins as an improvement. Time in steaming, 3 hours. [12]

HARD BISCUITS
Clarissa Lathrop
1823 Pittsfield Handwritten Receipe Book

1 pint milk
1 jill lard
6 teaspoons "yeast"
four teaspoons salt

Wet over night. Knead stiff when morning. Let rise, then bake.

BREAKFAST VANITIES

1 pint of flour
1 large teaspoonful of baking powder
½ teaspoonful of salt

Mix quite stiff with milk. Roll out, cut in squares and fry in hot lard like fritters. Serve with butter or syrup. [12]

FOR BREAKFAST

For Sunday morning in winter fry the hasty-pudding that was left over from Saturday night's supper. Eat it with West India molasses or Musovado sugar. In summer fried pudding is too heating. Pancakes with Cider and Sugar are better. Flapjacks are good on holidays or when the men folks are not working hard. Week day mornings farmers want some meat that can be cooked quickly, so as to let them go to the meadows before the sun is up. Sausages, Ham, Souse, fried Pork and eggs, or pork and apple with a milk gravy, with Irish potatoes boiled, are always handy. Salt Mackerel and Shad freshened over night and boiled are good. When the Shad catch comes, buy a Barrel of them and salt them yourself. They are very nice. Johnny cake or hoe cakes are a good change from Rye.[1]

GEMS

1 cup meal
1 cup flour
1 cup of sweet milk
½ cup of sugar
2 tablespoons of butter, melted

1 egg
1 teaspoonful of soda
2 teaspoonfuls of cream of tartar
A little salt [12]

BOILED POTATO YEAST

Three large, old potatoes, pared, soaked, and boiled until broken in small pieces: half a cup of loose hops boiled in one quart of water. Drain and mash the potatoes; add the hop water and enough more hot water to make two quarts. Strain, rubbing all the potato through, and put it on to boil. When boiling, add three fourths of a cup of flour, which has been wet to a smooth paste in cold water, and three quarters of a cup of sugar. Boil five minutes, stirring well; let it cool; add three fourths of a cup of yeast; and, when risen, add one fourth of a cup of salt. Keep in a covered stone jar in a cool cellar. Bread made with this yeast will not sour even in the hottest weather. [6]

—Mrs. Towne's Matilda

MUFFINS

2 cups of flour
4 teaspoons of baking powder
1 tablespoons of sugar
2 tablespoons melted fat

1¼ cups of milk
2 eggs
A pinch of salt

Beaten together for five minutes, bake in muffin tins 20 minutes. Makes one dozen. [12]

RICE GRIDDLE CAKES

Boil a cup of rice soft in four cups of milk. While warm, add a little flour. When cold, add three eggs and one teaspoon of salt. Fry as other griddle cakes. [9]

BUTTER DROPS

3 large tablespoons of butter
3 large tablespoons of sugar
½ cup sour milk
½ teaspoon of soda
2 cups of flour

Drop in buttered tins and bake quickly. [9]

SALLY LUNN

2 eggs
2 dessert spoons of sugar
Lump of lard the size of an egg
Lump of butter not quite as large
2 tablespoons of yeast
1 quart of flour

Mix with warm water to a soft dough and set to rise about ten in the morning, and it will be ready for tea. Twice working makes it lighter. [9]

Syrup for the Spring of the Year. - Boil together, dock root, thoroughwort, yarrow, mullein, sarsaparilla, coltsfoot, spearmint, May weed, dandelion root, and any other herbs you like. Boil down the water and add molasses to make a syrup. Put in brandy to keep. Make a good deal of this, and give all the family a tablespoonful before breakfast as a preventive of Spring fevers. [1]

YORKSHIRE PUDDING
to serve with hot Roast Beef.

Ingredients
1½ pint of milk, 6 large tablespoons of flour, 3 eggs, 1 saltspoonful of salt.

Mode
Put the flour into a basin with the salt, and stir gradually to this enough milk to make it into a stiff batter. When this is perfectly smooth, and all the lumps are well rubbed down, add the remainder of the milk and the eggs, which should be well beaten. Beat the mixture for a few minutes, and pour it into a shallow tin, which has been previously well rubbed with beef dripping. Put the pudding into the oven, and bake it for an hour; then, for another half hour, place it under the meat, to catch a little of the gravy that flows from it. Cut the pudding into small square pieces, put them on a hot dish, and serve. If the meat is baked, the pudding may at once be placed under it, resting the former on a small three-cornered stand.

Time
1½ hour. Average cost 7d.

SUFFICIENT for 5 or 6 persons. SEASONABLE at any time. [18]

PREFACE BREAD BREAKFAST CONTEMPORARY SOURCES

VILLAGE INN ORANGE BLOSSOM MUFFINS
Clifford Rudisill

This recipe was adapted from the original one offered by the Excelsior Hotel in Jefferson, Texas.

4 eggs, slightly beaten
1 cup granulated sugar
2 cups orange juice
8 tablespoons salad oil

8 cups muffin mix
2 cups orange marmalade
2 cups chopped pecans

Combine eggs, sugar, orange juice and salad oil. Add muffin mix and beat vigorously for about 30 seconds. Stir in marmalade and pecans. Fill greased muffin pans about ⅔ full. (Small muffin pans are best.) Bake at 400° for 20 to 25 minutes. Yields about 4 dozen muffins.

VILLAGE INN SCONES
Clifford Rudisill

This recipe was adapted from the original of John Tovey, owner and chef at Miller Howe Country House Hotel at Windermere in the Lake District of England, and given to the owners of the Village Inn by him in 1982 on their quest for the best scone recipe in England.

8 cups flour
1 teaspoon baking soda
1 tablespoon baking powder
1 lb. butter (softened)

1 teaspoon salt
7 tablespoons granulated sugar
10 eggs, lightly beaten
1 cup milk

Sift flour, salt, baking soda and baking powder together. Drop pinches of softened butter over flour. Blend gently with fingers until mixture resembles coarse cornmeal. Sprinkle with sugar and add lightly beaten eggs. Mix gentle with hands until well combined. Add milk to make pie dough consistency. Do not work too much. Pat out on floured table to form square, 1 inch thick. Cut into small triangles. (For browner scones, coat top with egg whites.)

Bake in 425° oven for about 18 minutes. Yields about 75 two-inch scones.

ZUCCHINI MORNING BREAD
Mary and Frank Newton, The Gables Inn, Lenox.

Comment: "Received raves when used in our restaurant."

1 cup sugar
½ cup oil
2 eggs
1 teaspoon baking powder
1 teaspoon salt
2 teaspoons baking soda

1 teaspoon vanilla
¼ teaspoon cinnamon
¼ teaspoon cloves
1 cup shredded zucchini
2 cups flour

Mix all ingredients, adding flour last. Bake in loaf pan at 400° for fifty minutes or until knife inserted comes out clean.

FRENCH TOAST
From the kitchen of Brook Farm

6 slices of Italian bread (about an inch thick)
4 eggs and 1 yolk
¼ cup heavy cream
½ teaspoon baking powder

Dissolve baking powder in cream. Beat eggs and yolk until frothy. Add cream and pinch of salt. Beat well again. Dip bread slices into mixture. Lay flat in dish with sides. Pour remaining egg mix over bread. Soak, turning often, for half an hour or until all egg is absorbed. (I do mine the night before, cover and refrigerate.) Heat vegetable oil, saute bread slices on both sides until crisp and brown. Drain well on paper towels.

Sprinkle with powdered sugar. Serve with butter and syrup. You can do four at a time in a 12 inch skillet. Also, these keep well in a low oven for about half an hour.

MILK TOAST
Mrs. Robert Ensign

A dish for an overtired and fractious child who needs to go to bed.

BREAD: Good white bread, preferably homemade and unsliced. (Squashy "Wonder" bread or equivalent will make a soggy mess of this dish.)
Milk
Butter
Pinch of Salt

Before preparing the milk toast, undress and bathe tired child, talking softly. When he is dressed for bed, seat him in his high chair while you make toast.
1. Slice 2 pieces of bread; leave crusts on.
2. Put ½ cup of milk in a sauce pan.
3. Heat milk to just under boiling point.
4. Toast bread until golden brown—not hard. Butter generously.
5. Place toast in a shallow chowder bowl and pour hot milk over it. Salt very lightly. Feed to your child quickly enough so that toast keeps somewhat intact. I have found that promising a small treat of reading, a song or game, or some tried-and-true popular diversion while feeding milk toast is helpful. This time-honored dish of hot, fresh, milky bread should slide down easily.

Pleasant dreams!

Note: One slice of toast may be enough. You know your child's appetite best. Using the right bowl can ensure the correct consistency. Too deep a bowl may make toast too wet. If you have only a deep bowl, use less milk.

DATE AND NUT BREAD
Zoa Campetti

1 one-pound package of dates
1½ cups boiling water
Cut up dates, cover with boiling water and set aside
1 cup walnut meats, broken and set aside also

In large mixing bowl, mix with a spoon:
1 tablespoons cooking oil
1¼ cups sugar
1 egg

2¾ cups all-purpose flour
2 tablespoons baking soda
dash of salt

Add date mixture to above ingredients and stir only with a spoon. Add broken walnuts and mix with spoon. Use two small bread tins which have been well greased and floured. Bake 1 hour at 350°—sometimes a bit longer. Cool on rack. Can be stored in foil; will last a long time if refrigerated.

GRIDDLE CAKES
Bertha Eddy

2 cups flour
2 tablespoons sugar
2 cups sour milk

1 tsp baking soda
2 eggs, separated
1 tsp salt

Sift flour with dry ingredients into bowl. Stir in sour milk and beat well. Add egg yolks and beat again. Fold in stiffly beaten egg whites. Cook in spoonfuls on hot, greased griddle until the bubbles formed on surface begin to break. Turn with a spatula and continue cooking until cakes begin to steam and are brown on bottom. Serve with butter and maple syrup. Makes 16 cakes.

N.B. Cultured buttermilk is a satisfactory substitute for sour milk. Blueberries may be sprinkled on top as soon as batter is spooned onto griddle. They will be incorporated into the griddlecakes (pancakes) when turned. Part whole wheat flour may be substituted if desired. A teflon lined electric frying pan or griddle will allow these griddlecakes (pancakes) to be cooked at the table.

HILLSDALE HOUSE GRAHAM BREAD
Edna B. Garnett

My mother's recipe from her aunt, Charlotte Sweat, who ran the Hillsdale House in Hillsdale, New York at the turn of the century.

1 egg
dash of salt
1 tablespoons shortening
½ cup sugar
½ to ⅔ cup molasses
1 cup white flour
1 cup graham flour
1 teaspoon soda
3 teaspoons baking powder
⅔ cup raisins*
chopped nuts*

*Optional

Mix together all ingredients except flour, soda and baking powder. Add flour, soda and baking powder. Knead in raisins and nuts last. Bake in a loaf pan at 375 to 400° for fifty minutes to one hour.

BERKSHIRE MUFFINS
Pat Shively

½ cup corn meal
½ cup flour
½ cup cooked rice
2 tablespoons sugar
3 teaspoons baking powder
½ teaspoon salt
⅔ cup scalded milk
1 egg
1 tablespoon melted butter.

Turn scalded milk on meal, let stand five minutes; add rice, and flour mixed and sifted with remaining dry ingredients. Add yolk of egg well beaten, butter, and white of egg beaten stiff and dry.

N.B. This recipe is of interest because of its name. Two possible modifications might be made: the hot milk should be poured over the corn meal and stirred well and the amount of baking powder might be cut to two teaspoons. The batter should be distributed in a muffin tin filling each buttered or greased cup approximately ½ full and baked in a preheated, hot oven for about 20 minutes.

SOPHIE'S PLAIN MUFFINS
Pat Schively

These were Sophie Swenson's from her days as the Salisbury's cook, at Tor Court, Pittsfield.

1 large spoon butter
½ cup sugar
1 egg
½ cup milk
1 cup flour
1 heaping teaspoon baking powder

Make quickly. Bake in hot oven 6 to 10 minutes. Makes 12.

(N.B. I set oven at 400°. Texture is not right if they bake more than ten minutes. Chopped pecans or blueberries can also be added.)

TABLE OF CONTENTS   BOOK I   SEAFOOD   OLD SOURCES

Then Stubb finished the steak, saying, "Well, then, cook, you see this whale-steak of yours was so very bad, that I have put it out of sight as soon as possible; so you see that don't you? Well, for the future, when you cook another whale steak for my private table here, the capstan, I'll tell you what to do so as not to spoil it by overdoing. Hold the steak in one hand, and show a live coal to it with the other; that done, dish it' d'ye hear? And now tomorrow cook, when we are cutting in the fish, be sure you stand by to get the tips of his fins; have them put in pickle. As for the ends of the flukes, have them soused, cook. There, now ye may go."

MELVILLE, *MOBY-DICK*

CREAMED OYSTERS

A pint of cream, one quart of oysters, a small piece of onion, a very little mace, a tablespoonful of flour, and salt and pepper to taste. Let the cream, with the onion and mace, come to a boil. Mix flour with a little cold milk or cream, and stir into the boiling cream. Let the oysters come to a boil in their own liquor, and skim carefully. Drain off all the liquor, and turn the oysters into the cream. Skim out the mace and onion, and serve. Very nice. [2]

SCALLOP FRITTERS
Mrs. Walter E. Hall

1 qt. Scallops
scant ½ pint milk
1 teaspoon salt
1 pint. sifted flour
1 tablespoon melted butter
2 eggs

Wash and drain scallops, season with salt and pepper, mix with following batter: sifted flour, milk, melted butter, salt and eggs. Beat eggs briskly, add milk. Beat again and pour mixture on flour. Then add butter and salt. Stir in scallops. Drop spoonful at a time of mixture into boiling fat. Cook a nice brown. Drain on brown paper and serve very hot. [12]

CHICKINS FORC'D WITH OYSTERS
(Taken from a receipt book written in 1764.)

Take Oysters, parsley, onions, butter, pepper, salt, grated bread, mushrooms—if you can get y'm, & as many eggs as you think proper, fill them inside, & cut y'm on the breast, if you have a mind to, & put some of the stuffing there, make gravy of Oysters, butter & mace, pepper, roast them well.

LOBSTER A LA NEWBURG

One and one-half cups lobster meat, chopped fine; one tablespoonful butter, three-fourths cupful maderia or sherry, one cupful cream, yolks of two eggs, one truffle chopped, one-fourth teaspoon salt, dash of cayenne or paprika. Put butter in saucepan until melted. Add lobster, truffle, salt, pepper; cover, let it simmer five minutes. Add wine; cook three minutes longer. Have yolks and cream well beaten together and add this to lobster. Shake the sauce pan until mixture thickens. Serve immediately. [8]

LOBSTER CUTLETS

One lobster chopped fine. Cream two tablespoons butter and one and one-half tablespoons flour together on stove. Add one cup bouillon or one-half pint of cream. Cook five minutes. Add chopped lobster. Season with pepper and salt and add yolk of one egg. Let cool; shape into cutlets. Dip in egg and roll in bread crumbs. Fry in deep fat and garnish with claw of lobster in end of each cutlet. [8]

LOBSTER SALAD

Two lobsters picked fine, four heads of fresh lettuce cut fine, put in a dish in layers with the lobsters; boil your eggs, mash the yolks, add three tablespoons of melted butter, and a teaspoon of mustard, cayenne pepper and salt; two tablespoons of sugar, two cups of vinegar. When boiling hot pour over salad and serve. [9]

SCALLOPED OYSTERS
Mrs. A.B. Mole

Two quarts of oysters, half a cup of butter, half a cup of cream or milk, four teaspoonfuls of salt, half a teaspoonful of pepper, two quarts of stale bread crumbs, and spice if you choose. Butter the scallop dishes and put in a layer of crumbs and then one of oysters, dredge with the salt and pepper and put small pieces of butter here and there in the dish. Now have another layer of oysters, seasoning as before, then add the milk, and finally, a thick layer of crumbs, which dot with butter. Bake twenty minutes in a rather quick oven. The crumbs must be light and flaky. The quantity given will fill two dishes. [2]

FRICASSEED OYSTERS

Drain a quart of large oysters from their liquor, and place them in a covered saucepan with a quarter of a pound of good butter. Set them on the back of the range, and let them simmer gently till the oysters are well plumped out. Put the oyster liquor in another saucepan with three tablespoons of powdered cracker and a little pepper. When the oysters are done, remove them from the butter with a fork, and place them on toasted crackers on a hot platter. Add the butter in which they have been cooked to the oyster broth. Let it boil up once. Stir in half a pint of cream, and pour over the oysters. [16]

PICKLED OYSTERS

Scald the oysters in their own liquor, with a little water added, until they are plump. Skim them out, and drop into a bowl of cold water; rinse well and put them in glass jars.

Scald an equal quantity of the liquor and vinegar with whole peppers, mace, and salt, and when perfectly cold fill the jars up with it. These will keep two or three weeks. [16]

A Quaker Stew is good for an inflamed throat and itching cough. Take a piece of butter the size of a shagbark, a pint of molasses, a little vinegar and a dash of red pepper. Boil until it strings. Take hot or cold in doses to suit. [1]

A Slice of Salt Pork spread with pepper and bound on with a strip of red flannel will cure a sore throat. Or, in a pinch, a stocking taken warm from the foot and bound about the throat is efficacious. [1]

OYSTERS ON A CHAFING-DISH

Put into the chafing-dish four or five tablespoons of the oyster liquor; add salt, white pepper, and a tablespoonful of butter, and stir till it is scalding hot. Drop the oysters in, a dozen at a time, and cook till they are plump and tender; then skim out and place on slices of hot buttered toast; add more oysters as required.[16]

FINNAN HADDIE

Finnan Haddie may be broiled, baked in milk, fried, steamed, and creamed. A favorite recipe is to cut the fish in large pieces and plunge into boiling, unsalted water. Simmer 10 or 15 minutes. Drain, and when cool enough pick apart with a fork, mashing as fine as possible. Add a little cream, taking care not to make it "sloppy." Dash of pepper, and butter half the size of an egg (more or less according to quantity of fish). Heat the mixture until the ingredients are thoroughly blended, then spread on rounds of fried bread, or points of toast. Pile the fish high in the centre, and heat or slightly brown in oven.[12]

CREAMED SHRIMPS BAKED WITH GREEN PEPPERS
Mrs. Walter E. Hall

12 even-sized green peppers
¼ teaspoon pepper
⅛ teaspoon celery seed
1 cup fine bread crumbs

2 tablespoons butter
1 teaspoon mixed mustard
1 beaten egg
1 qt. shrimp

Remove the stems and seeds of the green peppers and soak in cold water ¾ hr. Drain and stuff with the following mixture: Cream 2 tablespoons butter and thoroughly mix with ¼ teaspoon pepper, 1 teaspoon mixed mustard, ⅛ teaspoon celery seed, and 1 beaten egg.

When mixed stir in 1 cup fine bread crumbs. Then add 1 qt. shrimps. Should the shrimps be fresh—not canned ones—you will need to season the sauce with salt. Fill each pepper with the mixture, sprinkle with fine bread crumbs and pieces of butter, and bake in quick oven for 15 minutes. [12]

CODFISH AND CREAM

Shred two thirds of a bowlful of salt codfish, wash it several times with fresh water, drain off the water, and put it into a saucepan with a pint of sweet cream and half a pint of sweet milk. Let it come nearly, but not quite, to the boiling point. Beat together one egg, a tablespoonful of flour, and two tablespoons of sweet milk; add it to the fish, and stir continually until it is done. Put the mixture in a hot dish, and add a large spoonful of butter, stirring it thoroughly. [16]

Adapting eighteenth and nineteenth-century recipes is an exciting adventure. Guidelines calling for "a wine glass of . . ." "two porringers of . . .", "as much mace as needed, "boil at 2 or 3 wollops," all add to the confusion of translating these delights into workable twentieth century cooking. [21]

For Chin Cough or Whooping Cough. Rub the chin lying down with old Rum. It seldom fails. Or give a spoonful of juice of Pennyroyal mixed with brown Sugar candy. [1]

FRIED COD FISH

Soak cod fish over night in cold water. Cut in pieces about two inches square, roll in Indian meal and fry with salt pork.[1]

FISH BALLS - Maine

Soak over night three quarters of a pound of boneless codfish. In the morning shred the fish (uncooked) very carefully with silver fork till it is fine. Add to it a dozen potatoes of medium size, freshly boiled, mashed, and rubbed through a sieve, two beaten eggs, a tablespoonful of butter, a little hot milk or cream, and a sprinkling of white pepper. Mold into round balls, and drop into very hot fat.[16]

SOLES NORMANDE

Take the fillets from three fine soles, fold them in two, and lay them in a buttered, flat saucepan, with half a glassful of white wine, three tablespoons of mushroom liquor, and half a pinch each of salt and pepper. Cover and cook for six minutes; then lift them up, drain, and arrange them on a dish. Reduce the gravy to one-half, add twelve blanched oysters, and six sliced mushrooms, moistening with half a pint of Allemande sauce. Thicken the sauce well with a tablespoonful of good butter, tossing well till dissolved, and add the juice of half a lemon. Garnish the sides of the dish with the oysters and mushrooms, pour the sauce over the fish. Decorate with three small, cooked crawfish, three fried smelts, and three small, round croquetts of potatoes.[4]

GUMBO FILÉ—A New Orleans Dish

50 oysters
1 fowl cut into pieces
½ pound of veal cut into pieces
½ pound of ham cut into pieces
3 tablespoons of tomato
1 tablespoonful of drippings
2 tablespoons of sassafrass powder

2 onions
½ teaspoonful of salt
¼ teaspoonful of pepper
¼ teaspoonful of powdered thyme
¼ teaspoonful of marjoram
Dash of cayenne

Wash well the outside of a fowl, and cut it into pieces. Cut the veal and the ham into small pieces, and dredge all of them well with flour.

Put the onions, sliced, into a pot or large saucepan with one tablespoonful of fat or drippings, and fry until brown; then add the pieces of chicken, veal, and ham. Turn them often, so all will brown evenly; this will take about twenty minutes. When the meat is browned, add two quarts of hot water; cover the pot, and let simmer for two hours. After the first hour add the salt, pepper, thyme, marjoram, and tomatoes. At the end of two hours, if the meat is tender, add the oysters and the oyster juice, and let remain on the fire only long enough to ruffle the gills of the oysters. Take from the fire, and add two tablespoons of sassafras powder, and stir until a little separate.[16]

Camomile for Consumption.
The attention of a young lady, apparently in the last stage of consumption, was called to the virtue of camomile by observing from her window early each morning, a dog with scarcely any flesh on his bones go and lick the dew of a maomile bed in the garden, in doing which the animal was noticed to alter his appearance, to recover his strength, and finally looked plump and well.[1]

SOLES AU GRATIN

Put three tablespoons of cooked, fine herbs in the bottom of deep baking dish, fold the fillets in two, and place them in, crown-shaped. Season with half a pinch each of salt and pepper, then moisten with half a glassful of white wine, and bake for five minutes. Take out the dish, decorate it with twelve mushroom buttons, adding half a pint of good Espagnole sauce. Sprinkle over with fresh bread-crumbs, pour on a few drops of melted butter, and bake once more for three minutes, then press the juice of half a lemon over the fillets, add half a pinch of chopped parsley, and serve. (All fish au gratin are prepared the same way.) [4]

FROGS A L'ESPAGNOLE

Trim nicely eighteen fine, fresh, medium-sized frogs' feet; lay the frogs in a sautoire on the hot stove with two ounces of good butter, season with a pinch of salt and half a pinch of pepper, and add half a glassful of white wine. Let cook for five minutes, then put in it half an empty green pepper and two freshly peeled tomatoes, all cut up into small pieces; cook for ten minutes longer, then dress the frogs on a hot dish, and send to the table. [4]

SCALLOPS BRESTOISE

Blanche one pint of scallops in one ounce of butter for ten minutes, and then drain; chop up two onions, and put them in a saucepan with an ounce of butter; when brown add one tablespoonful of flour, stirring carefully, and moisten with half a pint of the scallop liquor; if none, white broth will answer. Let reduce while stirring, then season with a good pinch of salt, and half a pinch of white pepper, also a very little cayenne pepper; add the chopped scallops, four egg yolks, and a bruised clove of garlic, also half a cupful of fresh bread-crumbs, and a tablespoonful of chopped parsley. Stir well for two minutes, then put it in a dish and lay aside to cool. Fill six scallop-shells, or St. Jacques-shells with this. Besprinkle the tops with fresh bread-crumbs, moisten slightly with clarified butter, and lay them on a baking-sheet; brown them nicely in the oven for five minutes, and serve on a hot dish with a folded napkin garnished with parsley-leaves.[4]

TROUT WITH FINE HERBS

Clean, wash, and dry six fine trout, of a quarter of a pound each. Put them on a buttered dish, adding half a glassful of white wine and one finely chopped shallot. Let cook for ten minutes, then put the gravy in a saucepan, with two tablespoons of cooked herbs moistening with half a pint of Allemande sauce. Reduce the gravy to one-half, and pour it over the trout with the juice of half a sound lemon, and serve.[4]

For Hydrophobia.
Wash oyster shells, put them on a bed of live coals and burn. Powder and sift fine. Take three tablespoons of this powder, add a sufficiency of egg to make a soft dough and fry in a little butter. Let the patient eat this cake in the morning, and abstain from food and drink for six hours. This dose repeated for three mornings is in all cases sufficient.[1]

CRABS Á la ST. LAURENT

Reduce half a pint of good velouté with half a glassful of white wine, season with one pinch of salt, half a pinch of pepper, and a very little cayenne pepper, adding three tablespoons of grated Parmesan cheese. Take three-quarters of a pound of shelled crabs, put them in the saucepan, and boil them for ten minutes; then lift from the fire and let cool. Prepare six squares of toasted bread, and with a knife spread some of the mixture smoothly over each slice, sprinkle well with grated cheese, and moisten slightly with clarified butter; place them on a baking-dish; bake in a very hot oven for three minutes, and serve on a hot dish with a folded napkin, garnished with parsley-greens.[4]

TABLE OF CONTENTS BOOK I SEAFOOD CONTEMPORARY SOURCES

GRAVAD LAKS - CURED SALMON GRAVLAX
Jytte Brooks

Yield Portion—6 - 8
Preparation Time—15 minutes
Cooking Time—48 - 72 hrs.
Oven Temperature—refrigeration

1 6-8 lb (3 kg) whole salmon
½ cup (150 g) kosher salt
½ cup (150 g) sugar
2 tablespoons (20 g) white peppercorns
1 cup (40 g) fresh dill or 8 sprigs

Remove head, tail and fins from salmon. Clean, debone and cut into two fillets. Make sure all bones have been removed. Arrange one fillet skin side down on a plastic sheet in a dish (a fish poaching pan is a perfect size). Cover the entire fillet with dill, coarsely ground white pepper, salt and sugar. Place the second fillet on top of it, flesh side down and wrap fillets in plastic. Use only half of salt/sugar mixture for one fillet. A board and heavy cans should be arranged on top of the fish for weight.

Refrigerate for 48 to 72 hours, turning every 12 hours. Remove fillets and scrape them clean. Place the fillet on a board and with a sharp knife, slice the fish thinly crosswise on a slant. Serve with dill sauce and garnish with dill and lemon slices. Gravlax will keep refrigerated for at least one week.

PAELLA
Fran Dichter

1-½ lb. lobster
1 lb. shrimp
1 dozen small clams or 1 lb. mussels
1-½ chicken
1 teaspoon oregano
2 peppercorns
1 glove garlic
salt
6 tablespoons. olive oil
1 teaspoon vinegar
* (2 oz. sliced ham cut in strips)
  (½ lb. chorizo-hot Spanish sausage)

1 onion peeled and chopped
1 green pepper, chopped
½ teaspoon ground coriander
1 teaspoon capers
3 tablespoons tomato sauce
1 cup rice
2 to 3 cups boiling water
1 teaspoon saffron (or 1 teaspoon tumeric)
frozen peas
1 can pimentos, if desired

*Recipe calls for chorizo and sliced ham, added with the onions and pepper. This can be omitted.

Remove meat from lobster, clean shrimp, mussels and clams. Cut chicken into serving-size pieces.

Combine oregano, peppercorns, garlic, salt, 2 tablespoons olive oil and mash with spoon. Rub chicken with this mixture.

Heat remaining oil in deep skillet. Brown chicken quickly, over moderate heat. Add onion, green pepper, coriander and capers. Cook five minutes over low heat. Add tomato sauce and rice and cook five minutes. Add boiling water, saffron and shrimp. Mix well, and cook rapidly, covered, until the liquid is absorbed (about 20 minutes). Place this in ovenproof serving dish. Add lobster meat and peas and cook 5 minutes longer (preferably in oven at 350°). Steam mussels and clams until shells open. Heat pimentos and drain. Use mussels and clams as garnish along with pimentos. Add some of the liquid shellfish were cooked in. This broth adds to the flavor. Serves 6 to 8.

BAKED BLUEFISH BRESLIN (About 4 lb.)
Ted Giddings

Place on well-buttered baking pan or oven-proof platter. Bake 20 minutes at 400°. Mix following:

2 egg yolks
2 tablespoons chopped pickle
2 tablespoons chopped parsley
2 tablespoons lemon juice

1 tb. vinegar
½ teaspoon salt
½ teaspoon paprika

Spread above over fish. Continue baking until fish flakes when tried with fork. (About 30 minutes.) Serves 6 to 8.

SHAD ROE (Broiled)
Ted Giddings

Parboil in boiling salted water for 10 minutes. Put on broiling pan. Cover with bacon strips. Broil until bacon is done.

BAKED OR PLANKED SHAD
Ted Giddings

Put shad in shallow baking dish or on buttered plank, skin side down. Sprinkle with salt and pepper. Brush with melted butter.

Bake 25 minutes at 400°. Spread with butter, chopped parsley and lemon. 3 lbs. of shad serves 6.

SHRIMP CREOLE
Frances Vaughan

Make a dark roux of:
¼ cup flour
¼ cup bacon grease

in a large heavy pot. Add:

1-½ cups chopped onions
1 cup chopped green onions
1 cup chopped celery with leaves
1 cup chopped bell pepper
2 cloves garlic, minced

and saute until soft. Add following ingredients:

1 six-ounce can tomato paste
1 16 oz. can chopped tomatoes with liquid
1 8 oz. can tomato sauce
1 cup water
5 teaspoons salt
1 teaspoon pepper

½ teaspoon red pepper (optional)
Tabasco sauce to taste
2 to 3 bay leaves
1 teaspoon sugar
1 teaspoon Worcestershire sauce
1 tablespoon lemon juice

Simmer slowly for one hour, covered, stirring occasionally. Add 4 pounds peeled raw shrimp. Cook until done, 5 to 15 minutes. This should set awhile and is much better made the day before and reheated but not boiled. Freezes well.

Add just before serving: ½ cup chopped parsley. Remove bay leaves before serving. Serve over 2 to 3 cups cooked rice.

ALICE'S SPECIAL SHRIMP
Alice Brock

"This dish was inspired by a recipe of Karl Lipsky's. Karl is one of the great unsung cooks of the Berkshires. This became very popular at Alice's at Avaloch. Originally, I created it for visual appeal, but in addition to the colors, I wanted various flavors and textures that would retain their individuality and, of course, end up tasting great together."

For each person:
5 large raw shrimps, peeled and de-veined
4 black olives
4 green olives
4 ripe cherry tomatoes
4 artichoke hearts
1 handful of roughly chopped scallions and parsley
½ heaping teaspoon of Tarragon
1 to 3 tablespoons of butter
3 to 4 tablespoons of sherry

For 2 people, use a 10-inch frying pan; for 4 people use at least a 12-inch frying pan.

Melt butter. Turn heat to high; add sherry and all ingredients except shrimp. Bring to a boil to cook off alcohol. Add shrimp, turning once until JUST cooked. Serve over orzo (a rice-shaped pasta).

TABLE OF CONTENTS BOOK II POULTRY OLD SOURCES

Don't you think you can say which is the dark-meat and which is the white-meat poet? And so of the people you know; can't you pick out the full-flavored, coarse-fibred characters from the delicate, fine-fibred ones? And in the same person, don't you know the same two shades in different parts of the character that you find in the wing and thigh of the partridge? I suppose you poets may like white meat best, very probably; you had rather have a wing than a drumstick, I dare say.

—Why, yes,—said I,—I suppose some of us do. Perhaps it is because a bird flies with his white-fleshed limbs and walks with the dark-fleshed ones. Besides, the wing-muscles are nearer the heart than the leg-muscles.

OLIVER WENDELL HOLMES,
POET AT THE BREAKFAST TABLE

CHICKEN SOUFFLE

1 tablespoonful of butter
1 tablespoon of flour
1 tablespoon of chopped parsley
1 cupful of milk
1 cupful of minced chicken

½ teaspoonful of salt
3 eggs
10 drops of onion juice
Dash of pepper

Make a white sauce by putting the butter in a saucepan or double boiler. When melted add the flour, and cook a moment without browning. Then add slowly the milk, and stir till smooth. Season with salt, pepper, parsley, and onion juice. There should be one cupful of the sauce. Remove from the fire, and stir in the beaten yolks of three eggs; then add a cupful of chicken chopped fine. Stir the mixture over the fire a minute until the egg has a little thickened; then set aside to cool.

Rub a little butter over the top, so it will not form a crust. When time to serve beat very stiff the whites of the three eggs, and stir them lightly into the cold chicken mixture. Put it into a pudding dish, and bake in hot oven for twenty minutes. Serve at once in the same dish. This is a soufflé, so the whites of the eggs must not be added until it is time for it to go into the oven, and it will fall if not served immediately after it comes from the oven. This dish may be made with any kind of meat. Chicken soufflé may be baked in paper boxes, and served as an entreé.[16]

CHICKEN SOUFFLE
Mrs. Charles W. Wright

Two cups scalded milk, one-fourth cup butter, one-fourth cup flour, one teaspoonful salt, one-fourth teaspoonful pepper, one-half cup stale bread crumbs, two cups cold chopped chicken, yolks of three eggs well beaten. Make sauce of first ingredients, then add crumbs; cook three minutes; remove from fire; add chicken, yolks of eggs; fold in well beaten whites last. Bake in pudding dish 35 minutes, and serve hot with mushroom sauce.

Mushroom sauce: Two tablespoons butter, two tablespoons flour, one cup water, salt and pepper, one-fourth can sliced mushrooms. Cook two minutes. [8]

CHICKEN CROQUETTES
Mrs. A.W. Hunter

One-half pound of chicken, chopped very fine and seasoned with one-half teaspoonful of salt, one-half teaspoonful of celery salt, one quarter saltspoonful of cayenne pepper, one saltspoonful of white pepper, a few drops of onion juice, one teaspoonful of chopped parsley and one teaspoonful of lemon juice. Make one pint of very thick cream sauce. When thick, add one beaten egg and mix the sauce with the chicken, using only enough to make it soft as can be handled. Spread on shallow plate to cool. Shape; roll in fine bread crumbs, beaten egg, crumbs again. Fry one minute in smoking hot fat.[8]

ROAST GOOSE

Green geese about four months old are the best, as they get very tough when much older. If there is any doubt about the age of the goose, it is better to braise than to roast it. It can be browned after it is braised, and have the same appearance as if roasted. Dress and truss a goose the same as turkey; singe and wash the skin well; flatten the breast bone by striking it with a rolling-pin. Stuff it only partly full with mashed potato highly seasoned with onion, sage, salt, and pepper, or with a mixture of bread, apples, sage, salt, and pepper, and a thick coating of flour; put a little water in the pan and baste frequently. Allow eighteen minutes to the pound for a young goose, twenty-five minutes for an older one. Serve with goose apple sauce and a brown giblet gravy.[16]

TAME DUCKS

Prepare the same as geese. Stuff with the same mixture or with celery. Roast ducklings in hot oven twenty minutes, if liked rare; thirty minutes if they are to be cooked through. Old ducks require an hour to cook, and should be basted frequently. Pekin ducks, a breed of white ducks raised in quantities on Long Island, are especially esteemed.[16]

ROAST GOOSE, STUFFED WITH CHESTNUTS, APPLE SAUCE

Have a fine, tender goose of four pounds, singe, draw, wash well, and thoroughly wipe the interior with a cloth; then fill it with some stuffing as for the turkey. Close both ends, truss well, sprinkle a pinch of salt over, envelop in buttered paper and put it into a roasting-pan. Cook it for one hour and a half in a moderate oven, basting it occasionally with the drippings. Remove from the oven, dress on a hot serving-dish, untruss, skim off the fat from the gravy, add to it a gill of white broth, let come to a boil, then strain the gravy into a sauce-bowl and serve separately.[4]

CHICKEN PIE
Mrs. C.H. Cutting

Boil the chicken until tender. With the water in which it was boiled make a gravy, allowing one-half cup of flour and two tablespoons of butter to every quart of water. Season with pepper and salt; put in baking dish; add chicken, from which bones have been removed; cover with one-half pint of cream and pieces of butter; cover with a rich pie crust and bake one hour.

TURKEY BREASTS Á LA ROBINSON

Cook for twenty minutes, take it off and place it in another saucepan. Baste it with its own gravy, adding half a pint of Espagnole sauce. Blanch half a pint of chicken or turkey livers, cut them into two or three pieces according to their size, and put them with the turkey, adding half a glassful of Madeira wine. Let cook for twenty minutes more, and serve with the livers around the breasts, and the gravy thrown over.[4]

SQUABS ROASTED PLAIN

Singe, draw, cut off the necks, wipe neatly, and truss six fine, small squabs; put them in a roasting-pan with half a pinch of salt, evenly divided, and a very little butter spread over. Put the pan into a brisk oven to cook for twelve minutes; then remove from the oven untruss, and dress them on a hot dish, on which you have previously placed six small canapes, one on each canape; neatly decorate the dish with fresh watercress; skim the fat from the gravy, add to it a gill of white broth; let it just come to a boil, strain it into a sauce-bowl, and send to the table separately.[4]

Simple Headache Cure. - Take a quantity of black pepper and put it in a handkerchief; then fold the handkerchief over so that the grains cannot fall out, and saturate the whole thing with camphor; bind this plaster on the head and lie down. In a very few minutes the headache will be relieved, and the patient will be asleep. When the handkerchief becomes dry, saturate again with camphor.[8]

PIGEON CUTLETS A LA VICTORIA

Singe, draw, and bone three fine pigeons, leaving on the legs; cut them in two, and stuff lightly with chicken forcemeat, immerse them in beaten egg and fresh breadcrumbs, then cook in a sautoire with half an ounce of clarified butter, for four minutes on each side, and serve with half a pint of hot Victoria sauce on the warm dish, and the cutlets on top, with paper ruffles nicely arranged.[4]

CHICKEN SALAD

One large chicken cooked and picked fine, three heads of celery, yolks of four eggs, well beaten, two spoonfuls mixed mustard, six tablespoons of vinegar, one teaspoon of pepper, and one of salt; mix well and set into boiling water, stirring constantly until it thickens.[9]

FRICASSEED CHICKEN

Joint the chicken and boil gently till tender. When done fry slices of salt pork to a delicate brown, take from the fry-pan and arrange on platter. Put the chicken, which has meantime been draining, into the pan and brown in the pork fat.

Thicken the chicken broth with flour mixed smooth with water, add some butter the last thing, pour part of this gravy over the chicken which has been placed on the platter with the pork around it. The rest of the gravy should be poured over toast in another dish.[1]

CHICKEN CUTLETS (An Entree).

Ingredients. - 2 chickens; seasoning to taste of salt, white pepper, and cayenne; 2 blades of pounded mace, egg and bread crumbs, clarified butter, 1 strip of lemon-rind, 2 carrots, 1 onion, 2 tablespoons of mushroom ketchup, thickening of butter and flour, 1 egg.

Mode. - Remove the breast and leg bones of the chickens; cut the meat into neat pieces after having skinned it, and season the cutlets with pepper, salt, pounded mace, and cayenne. Put the bones, trimmings, &etc., into a stewpan with 1 pint of water, adding carrots, onions, and lemon-peel in the above proportion; stew gently for 1½ hour, and strain the gravy. Thicken it with butter and flour, add the ketchup and 1 egg well beaten; stir it over the fire, and bring it to the simmering-point, but do not allow it to boil. In the meantime, egg and bread-crumb the cutlets, and give them a few drops of clarified butter; fry them a delicate brown, occasionally turning them; arrange them pyramidically on the dish, and pour over them the sauce.

Time. - 10 minutes to fry the cutlets. Average cost, 2s each. Sufficient for an entree. Seasonable from April to July. [22]

A drop of peroxide of hydrogen will immediately remove a blood stain in a clean collar, gown or shirt. [9]

BRAISED CHICKEN

A fowl too old to roast may be made tender and good by braising, and present the same appearance as a roasted chicken.

Prepare it as for roasting, trussing it into good shape. Cut into dice a carrot, turnip, onion, and stalk of celery; put them in a pot with a few slices of salt pork laid over the breast; add a bouquet of parsley, one bay-leaf, three cloves, six peppercorns, also a teaspoonful of salt, and a pint of hot water. Cover the pot closely and let simmer for three hours. If any steam escapes, a little more water may have to be added. When done, rub a little butter over the breast, dredge with flour, and place in the oven a few minutes to brown, season to taste, and if necessary thicken with a little brown roux; serve it with the chicken as sauce. [16]

FRIED CHICKEN

Cut a tender chicken in pieces; dip the pieces in water; sprinkle them with salt and pepper and roll them in flour; saute them in a tablespoonful of lard or butter, browning both sides; then remove and add to the pan a tablespoonful of flour; cook it for a minute without browning, stirring all the time, and add a cupful of milk or cream; stir until it is a little thickened; strain; mix into it a tablespoonful of chopped parsley. Place the sauce on the serving-dish and arrange the pieces of chicken on it.[16]

CHICKEN LOAF TO BE STEAMED OR BAKED
Mrs. S.M. Bernhard

Two cups of cooked chopped chicken using light and dark meat. 4 cups of bread crumbs moistened well with hot milk, 4 tablespoons butter, 3 teaspoons salt, ½ teaspoon pepper, 2 teaspoons onion juice. If desired one cup of cold cooked peas, asparagus, or other delicate vegetable. Mix the whole with two well beaten eggs, pack in buttered mold, cover with greased paper, steam for one hour or until firm in center, or bake in a slow oven. If baked remove paper last quarter hour and brown. Serve garnished with sliced tomatoes and riced potato or new potato balls.[12]

CHICKEN AND MACARONI
Mrs. R.M. Weisgarber

Boil chicken until tender. Take out all bones and pick meat fine. Boil ½ package macaroni till tender. Butter dish, put layer of macaroni, thin layer of chicken with dots of butter, pepper and salt till dish is full. Cover with liquor of chicken. Pour cup of cream over all and bake ½ hour. Serve with peas and celery.[12]

TABLE OF CONTENTS BOOK II POULTRY CONTEMPORARY SOURCES

CORNFLAKE CHICKEN
Lee Stanfield

Tom's all-time favorite since fried foods are restricted is what we call Corn Flake Chicken. Tom says this is as close to Southern Fried Chicken as we can come within his restrictions. Our summer neighbor Millie Tower gave me this recipe a couple of years ago.

Skinned and boned chicken breasts	Crushed Corn Flakes
7-Up soda	Melted margarine

Marinate chicken breasts in 7-Up soda for about 1 hour. Dip in crushed corn flakes, sprinkle with a little melted margarine. Bake at 350° for about ¾ of an hour.

CAROL'S CHICKEN
Jeff Biden

1 or 2 chickens cut into serving-size pieces and skinned
1 cup honey (if honey is thin and almost liquid, 1-¼ cup)
⅓ cup soy sauce
½ teaspoon ground sage
½ teaspoon rice vinegar, optional

1. Place rack in flat bottom wok or heavy skillet so it is about ½" above cooking surface.
2. Add about 2 tablespoons water to wok or skillet.
3. Place chicken on rack.
4. Mix honey, soy sauce and sage until blended. Add vinegar, if desired. Pour over chicken.
5. Cover. Cook slowly, allowing sauce to bubble up onto chicken. Turn chicken once near end of cooking. Add water as needed.
6. Cooking time, 1 to 1-½ hours. Less time and thinner honey gives chicken a light tasty coating. More time and thicker honey gives chicken a candy-like coating.
7. Serve over rice with sauce on side.
8. Leftover sauce gives good flavor to soups and to ranch-style salad dressings. Cold and cubed sauce is a tasty aspic garnish.

PECAN BREADED BREAST OF CHICKEN
Clifford Rudisill - Village Inn

Ingredients:
8 oz. boneless, skinless breast of chicken
2 oz. pecans, coarsely chopped
flour in which to dredge chicken
salt and ground white pepper to taste.

Sauce
1 tablespoon shallots
1 oz. white wine
2 oz. heavy cream
1 tablespoon Dijon mustard
1 tablespoon whole butter
juice from ½ small lemon
salt and white pepper to taste

Season the chicken breast and lightly coat with flour. Allow to set at room temperature for one minute until flour becomes sticky on surface of chicken. Dredge in coarsely chopped pecans. Barely cover the bottom of a small saute pan with clarified butter and place over heat. When very hot, add chicken and saute on each side until pecans begin to brown. Place in 375° oven briefly to finish cooking. When chicken is done, remove to holding pan. Add shallots and white wine with mustard and allow to cook briefly.

Add heavy cream. Bring to boil. Swirl in whole butter and finish with lemon juice, salt and white pepper. Place chicken in service plate and cover with the sauce. Serves one.

JEWELED CHICKEN
Karen Border

4-6 chicken breast halves, skinless and boneless
1 teaspoon curry powder
½ c. heavy cream

1 jar chutney (10 oz.) Maharanee or other brand
Salt and pepper

Coat chicken breast halves with flour; salt and pepper to taste. In frypan, saute breasts in butter about 5" per side. While frying, sprinkle 1 teaspoon (or more, to taste) of good curry powder on breasts. Remove chicken from pan and deglaze pan with ½ c. heavy cream, on low heat. Stir in the jar of chutney. Return chicken to pan and simmer 5" more. Can be done ahead and re-heated in microwave. Fruity, not too hot! Serve with rice/wild rice mix.

CHICKEN KIEV
Mary Anna Kershaw

¾ cup butter
½ cup fine dry bread crumbs
2 tablespoons grated Parmesan cheese
1 teaspoon each of basil and oregano leaves
1 garlic clove chopped fine

¼ teaspoon salt
8 chicken thighs
¼ cup dry white wine
¼ cup chopped green onion
¼ cup chopped parsley

Melt butter in heavy pan. On piece of wax paper, combine crumbs and spices. Dip chicken in melted butter, then roll in crumb mixture. Place in ungreased 9-inch baking pan and bake in center of 375° oven for 50 minutes. Add wine, onions and parsley to remaining butter. Pour butter sauce around and over chicken. Return to oven 3 to 5 minutes until sauce is hot. Serve on rice with sauce spooned over.

OVEN BARBECUED CHICKEN
Beverly Trowill

3-3 ½ lb. chicken, disjointed and skinned
1 cup water
½ cup catsup
3 tablespoons lt. brown sugar

1 tablespoon Worcestershire sauce
1 teaspoon salt
¼ teaspoon black pepper

Arrange chicken pieces in single layer in a roasting pan. Combine all ingredients and pour over chicken. Bake uncovered in a preheated oven (400°) for 1 hour, turning once during cooking. Delicious served over rice and very easy! Serves four.

CHICKEN-Willis
Beverly Willis

6 single skinned, boneless chicken breasts
2 cans Mushroom Soup
¾ cup sour cream (can be diet light)
½ cup cooking sherry
Paprika
Fresh linguini pasta for 6

Cut breasts into three strips each. Put into flat baking pan. Mix 2 cans mushroom soup (avoid Golden type) with sour cream and sherry (thin with water as needed—the mixture should be thick and without lumps). Cover breasts with sauce. Sprinkle paprika over sauce. Bake in oven at 350° for approximately 30 minutes. Boil linguini. Spoon mushroom sauce over chicken and linguini. Serve hot. Serves six.

CHICKEN-Baked with Orange Juice
Mrs. Robert H. Ensign

Chicken, broiler size, cut into serving pieces*
Bread crumbs
Garlic salt
Onions
Soy Sauce (preferably low sodium, as garlic salt provides enough)
1 can frozen orange juice (thawed)
Paprika

*If you require more than one chicken, increase other ingredients. However, 1 can of orange juice and soy sauce can do for 2 chickens if they are not too large.

Preheat oven to 300°. Place chicken in baking dish, skin side down. Sprinkle with bread crumbs, garlic salt, and thinly sliced onions. Mix about 2 tablespoons of soy sauce with undiluted, thawed can of orange juice. Pour over chicken. Sprinkle paprika over top. Cook slowly about 1½ hours in 300° oven, basting occasionally. When done, there should be a goodly amount of sauce. Serve with freshly cooked rice.

CHICKEN STEW
Norma J. Zullo

Chicken	Onions	Corn and any other desired vegetables
Garlic	1 can chicken broth	Chicken broth
Celery	Carrots	flour to thicken
Potatoes	Peas	

Brown onions, garlic, celery and chicken in large saucepan. While these are cooking, peel carrots, potatoes, and cut into small pieces. Add chicken broth and remove chicken while vegetables are cooking. De-bone chicken and break into small pieces. Return to pan with other frozen vegetables and leftover vegetables. Make a paste of flour and water to thicken.

CHICKEN PIE
Mary Mace (From old recipe of Jessie N. Mace)

1 large chicken or fowl	3 tablespoons melted butter or margarine	½ pint heavy cream
1 medium onion	2 tablespoons chicken fat	1 cup milk
1 stalk celery	2 cups + 3 tablespoons flour	1 egg
2 small carrots		

Remove all fat from chicken and reserve. Cut chicken into pieces, add chopped onion, celery, carrots and salted water to cover. Simmer slowly until meat is tender and slips easily from bone (1 to 1½ hours). Remove meat from bones, put into casserole and refrigerate. Crack bones, return to pot and simmer 2-3 hours more or until full flavored broth results. Strain. Meantime, render fat from chicken using heavy skillet over low heat; strain. Set oven to 375° or 425° (see baking instructions.)

Sauce: Make roux of melted butter, 3 tablespoons flour. Slowly add 3 cups chicken stock to make smooth stock, add 1 cup cream. (If made previous day, reheat before continuing with recipe). Season to taste. Pour over chicken and place in oven.

Crust: Stir to smooth batter: Flour, chicken fat, 1 egg, beaten light to which is added 1 cup milk. When casserole in oven is bubbling hard, spoon over chicken. Do not remove casserole from oven. Crust will suck into sauce. Bake 375° for 15-20 minutes.

NOTE: Make additional sauce from remaining broth using 1 tablespoon butter, margarine, 1 tablespoon flour and ⅓ cup cream for each cup of broth. Serve with the chicken pie.

CHICKEN GHIVETCH
(Hungarian Vegetable Stew)
Anonymous

Improves as it stands, as stews do. Serves four.

1 package two chicken breasts - boneless, skinless and cut into serving pieces.
*¾ cauliflower, separated into florets
2 large potatoes or 3 med. pared and diced into bite-size pieces.
2 large carrots
2 medium onions, sliced
1 red or green pepper, sliced
3 ribs celery cut into 1" diagonal slices
1 can (1 lb.) peeled tomatoes
2 cloves garlic, minced
1-½ teaspoons salt
½ teaspoon pepper
1-½ cups chicken broth (13.75 oz. can College Inn)
3 tablespoons chopped fresh dill or 1 tablespoon dried dill weed.

*If you like eggplant, use ½ cauliflower and ½ eggplant.

Place chicken and vegetables in 4 quart casserole. Sprinkle with salt and pepper. Add tomatoes and tomato liquid. Add garlic to chicken broth and pour over ingredients. Sprinkle with dill. Cover tightly and bake in 350° oven for two hours (stir after one hour).

MOM'S TURKEY GLOP
Anne Everest Wojtkowski

2 cans Campbell cream of mushroom soup
1 can mushrooms and juice
Sherry (cooking, regular or cream)
2 cups cut-up turkey or chicken meat

Fresh or dried parsley
4 oz. package slivered almonds
2 cups cooked rice

Empty the cans of mushroom soup into a 3 quart pot and place on stove on low heat. Add entire contents of can of mushrooms, stirring. Mix in about ½ cup sherry; add more or less, depending on consistency desired to serve over bed of rice. Stir in poultry and parsley, bringing stove temperature to medium-high until nearly boiling, immediately reduce stove temperature to lowest setting, stirring occasionally until ready to serve. Serve over bed of cooked rice and top with almonds. Serves four.

NOTE: I developed this recipe as a result of slightly overbaking a chicken when I was single and learning how to cook. My brother Wallie, and I shared an apartment in our single days. That evening we ate the leg portions. The next night, I was trying to figure out what to do with the somewhat dry white meat, and decided I needed to put it in some kind of sauce. What evolved was a result of using what I happened to have on hand that seemed like it might do. This has become a favorite family dish. I have often increased the recipe to serve 40 and it still works great.

SWEET CHICKEN WINGS
Robert Cooper

2-lb. package (about 10 wings) chicken wings
Cut each wing at joints (3 pieces) and throw away tip. Trim fat and excess skin from pieces with shears

Marinade:

½ cup soy sauce
⅓ cup brown sugar

½ cup white wine
¼ teaspoon garlic powder

¼ teaspoon ginger

Marinate wings overnight or longer. Cover shallow pan with aluminum foil, spread pieces on pan after "blotting" off excess marinade with paper towels. Bake at 375° for one hour, try to turn pieces at 30 minutes.

WILD RICE WITH SMOKED TURKEY AND ORANGES
Mrs. Robert Bardwell, Jr.

4 ounces (½ cup) uncooked wild rice
2 cups uncooked long-grain white rice
2 pounds smoked turkey, cut into ¼ inch julienne strips
5 oranges, peeled and sectioned (or mandarin canned)
1 bunch parsley, finely chopped
1 orange, sliced, and parsley sprigs for garnish

Vinaigrette:
1 teaspoon salt
1 teaspoon freshly ground pepper
1 + ½ tablespoons dijon mustard
¾ cup red wine vinegar
¾ cup olive oil and ½ cup salad oil

Cook the wild and white rice according to the package directions and set them aside to cool. Place the turkey, cubed oranges and chopped parsley in a bowl. Add both kinds of cooled rice and set aside. Combine the ingredients for the dressing and whisk to blend well. Pour over the turkey-rice mixture until rice is well coated. Serve the salad on lettuce leaves, garnish each portion with an orange slice and a sprig of parsley. Serves 10.

TABLE OF CONTENTS BOOK III MEAT OLD SOURCES

But no doubt the first man that ever murdered an ox was regarded as a murderer; perhaps he was hung; and if he had been put on his trial by oxen, he certainly would have been; and he certainly deserved it if any murderer does. Go to the meatmarket of a Saturday night and see the crowds of live bipeds staring up at the long rows of dead quadrupeds.

HERMAN MELVILLE, MOBY-DICK

SEA PIE

People call this Sea Pie because a Sea-captain told them how to make it. You put your pork or veal or birds or anything you happen to have to boil. Add a quart of sweet dried apples and salt and pepper. When it is most done pour in a cup of molasses and cover it with dumplings and cook until done.

NOTE—This was the favorite dish of "Uncle Oliver" Smith. During the last year of Uncle Oliver's life he was in miserable health. It became necessary for him to make a trip to Boston, a serious undertaking then. He said he felt too weak to go, but a seapie might set him up. So "Aunt Lois" who looked after him bestirred herself and found some sweet dried apples and made a pie and set it before him. Having partaken of it, he was so strengthened, he made his journey, and settled his business successfully. [1]

BRAWN

Six pounds soup meat or two houghs boiled very tender; chop and add salt, pepper, and sweet herbs. Tie tightly in a cloth overnight. The stock will make three good soups. Neck pieces will answer. To be sliced and eaten with vinegar for tea. Always boil an onion with mutton. It prevents the woolly taste. [9]

IRISH STEW

Cut the neck of mutton into pieces two and one half or three inches square. Put them into a saucepan with one tablespoonful of butter, and let them brown; stir frequently so they do not burn. When browned add enough water to cover them well, and two or three onions cut into pieces. Cover closely and let simmer two hours. Then add more water if necessary, some parboiled potatoes cut in two and a few slices of carrot, salt, and pepper to taste; cover and let cook one hour more. A teaspoonful of Worcestershire sauce is an improvement. The gravy must be quite thick, so too much water must not be used. The potatoes should be very soft, but not broken. [16]

[From a Dutch book, we learn of the provisioning of whalers.] And in this chapter it was headed "Smeer" or "Fat" that I found a long detailed list of the outfits for the larder and cellars of 180 sail of Dutch whalemen; from which list, as translated by Dr. Snodhead, I transcribe the following:

A PROVISIONS FOR WHALING VESSEL

400,000 lbs. of beef
60,000 lbs. Friesland pork
150,000 lbs. stock fish
550,000 lbs. of biscuit
72,000 lbs. of soft bread
800 firkins of butter
20,000 lbs. Texel & Leyden cheese
144,000 lbs. cheese (probably an inferior article)
550 ankers of Geneva
10,800 barrels of beer

HERMAN MELVILLE, *MOBY-DICK*

FORCE MEAT BALLS

Mix with one pound of chopped veal or other meat, one egg, a little butter or raw pork chopped fine, one cup or less of bread crumbs, the whole well moistened with warm water, or what is better, the water from stewed meat seasoned with salt and pepper; make in small balls and fry brown.[9]

FORCE MEAT BALLS FOR BLACK BEAN SOUP

Take cold meat, chop very fine, add flour enough to make it stick together in balls about the size of a walnut; roll in flour and fry until brown, and add to the soup just before it is served.[9]

HASH

Hash, if made properly, is good. Corned beef is best, but roast beef or beef steak will answer. Chop not too fine, and put with potatoes chopped, in proportion one-third meat to two-thirds potatoes. Put in spider and pour in sufficient boiling water to moisten thoroughly, salt, butter and pepper to taste. Cook slowly and sometime, brown on the bottom and serve with the brown layer on top.[9]

DRIED BEEF

Shave thin, put in spider of cold water; when scalding hot, pour off water and put in cream or milk, a piece of butter, flour enough to thicken two eggs. Unsmoked beef is desirable. Turn over bits of stale bread.[9]

A BOILED CALF'S HEAD

Have the head split open, and the gristle about the nose and eyes, and the eyes and ears, removed by the butcher. Wash thoroughly the head; remove the tongue and brains; parboil the brains, and set them aside with the tongue to use on another occasion. Blanch the head by putting it into cold water; when it comes to the boiling point, pour off the hot water, and cover it with cold water. When cold, rub it with lemon. Put it into boiling water, enough to cover it; add two tablespoons of vinegar or white wine, twelve peppercorns, one bay-leaf, one onion, one carrot, and a sprig of parsley. Cover the pot, and let boil for two hours, or until tender, but not ready to fall apart. When done, take out the bones carefully, and lay the meat on a baking dish in compact shape. Rub over the top with egg, sprinkle it with bread crumbs and bits of butter, and set in the oven to brown. Serve with it a Poulette or an Allemende sauce. Put any of the meat left over after being served in this manner into a mold; fill it up with water in which the head was boiled; season to taste. This will make a jellied meat very good to use with salad. The water from the pot will make a good soup. Four separate dishes can be made from one head, viz.: boiled calf's head, cold jellied calf's head, mock turtle soup, tongue and brains, with white, Poulette, or Vinaigrette sauce.[16]

A CALF'S HEAD WITH VINAIGRETTE SAUCE

After the calf's head is boiled as directed above, take it from the water, remove the meat, and press it into a square mold or tin, and let it get entirely cold. It can then be cut into uniform pieces. When ready to serve, heat some of the liquor in which the head was boiled, cut some long slices from the form of cold calf's head, lay them in the hot liquor to become hot only. Remove them carefully, and place them on a hot dish. Pour over them a Vinaigrette sauce.[16]

When frying pork chops, sprinkle Bell's Poultry seasoning on them. Very tasty. [9]

Before frying beefsteak, sprinkle a little sugar on both sides and it retains the juice better. [9]

BEEF CROQUETTES

Chop fine some cold beef, beat two eggs and mix with the meat and add a little milk, melted butter, and salt and pepper. Make into rolls and fry.[9]

BEEF STEW

Two or three pounds of chuck steak, cut into pieces about two inches square, put into a sauce-pan with a coffee cup of cold water. Put over fire when boiling; let it simmer for two hours. While simmering, tie up a bunch of herbs, composed of knotted marjoram, winter savory, and a little thyme; take them out before the dish is served. Of course, the stew must be stirred occasionally; do not skim off fat. This is an Italian dish, and is eaten in that country with plain, boiled macaroni and Parmesan cheese, or with salad.[9]

ROAST BEEF PIE

Cut the cold roast beef left from a previous meal into thin slices, lay them in a deep dish lined with a good puff paste, sprinkle over a little pepper and salt, put in a few slices of tomatoes, another layer of beef, and another of seasoning; cover the whole with paste and bake half an hour.[9]

COTTAGE PIE

Hannan A. Bailey

1 cup chopped meat
1 cup hot water or gravy
2 cups mashed potatoes
½ teaspoon salt

1 cup hot milk
1 tablespoon butter
A few grains of celery salt
⅛ teaspoon pepper

Put meat in casserole. Add salt and pepper and the hot water or gravy. Mix the remaining ingredients with mashed potato and spread on top of meat. Bake in hot oven until potato is brown.[12]

CREAMED VEAL WITH GREEN PEPPERS

Mrs. H.A. Stubbs

Veal
Green pepper
Butter

3 Tablespoons flour
Milk

Cut veal left over from roast or stew into cubes. Slice a greenpepper and cook about five minutes in several tablespoons of butter. Lift pepper from fat. Add to the fat in pan two or three tablespoons of flour, enough to thicken quantity of medium white sauce needed for the amount of veal used, stir till blended. Gradually add milk and stir till thickened. Then stir in veal and peppers, season to taste, and serve on toast.[12]

FOR HOUSEHOLDS

Meat and potatoes may be roasted under the gas flame in the lower oven with much less gas than it takes to bake them in the upper oven. Turn off the gas from oven burners several minutes before the baking is finished, since the iron will retain sufficient heat to finish the work. There is heat enough in the oven burner to scorch a meringue placed near them after the gas has been turned off entirely. Plan to use both ovens at the same time as far as possible. While roasting in the lower compartment bake anything requiring a moderate heat, or oven may be used for boiling. Have kettles brought to the boiling point before placing them in oven.[8]

FINNISH MEAT BALLS
Ida Lambert

¾ cup soft breadcrumbs
1 cup cream
1-½ lb. lean hamburger
1 onion, chopped
1 egg, beaten

2 teaspoon salt
½ teaspoon allspice
2 tablespoons butter
2 tablespoons flour
1-½ cup milk

Soak bread in half cup of cream. Mix together meat, onion and breadcrumbs. Add egg, salt and allspice and combine well. Shape into balls, a teaspoonful if served as an appetizer, or larger if for a main course. Melt butter in frying pan and brown meat balls on all sides. When all are done, remove meat balls from pan and brown the flour in the fat. Add remaining cream and milk to pan and stir until smooth, if mixture seems too thick, add a little water. Return meat balls to pan, cover and simmer gently for 25 minutes. [8]

CALF'S HEAD AND PLUCK

Soak the head in ashes and water, scald and scrape. It must be cleaned with great care. The head, heart and lights (lungs: archaic) should be boiled full two hours. One hour is enough for the pluck. The animal's heart, liver, lungs, and brains should be washed and put in a bag with a pounded cracker and a little sifted sage, and boiled an hour, then broken up with a knife, peppered, salted, and buttered and put in a bowl by themselves. Make a sauce of butter and flour and boiling water and serve with the head.[1]

SOUSE

Pigs feet, ears, skins, et., should be scalded and cleaned. Boil four or five hours, until very soft. Skim out and pack in a jar, throwing in cloves, salt, pepper, as it is put in. Put a plate and a weight on top. Pour over hot vinegar. Cut in slices, dip in flour, and fry brown.[1]

PICKLED PIG'S FEET

Scrape and wash the pig's feet, cover with salt and water; let stand two days then put in more salt and let stand two days more; boil about two hours, slip out the bones and pour vinegar over with a few cloves and a stick of cinnamon.[1]

MEAT LOAF
Mrs. H.A. Stubbs

2 lbs. of beef
2 lbs. veal
½ lb. fat salt pork
1 onion

1 teaspoon sage
1 cup bread crumbs
½ cup corn meal

Boil beef and veal until tender. Chop fine with ½ lb. fat saltpork, 1 onion, 1 teaspoon sage, salt and pepper to taste, scald ½ cup corn meal with some of the water meat was boiled in, 1 cup bread crumbs. Mix well and make quite moist with water meat was boiled in. Bake until nice and brown. This is nice sliced cold.[12]

"Pork is an unwholesome meat, and should never be eaten by children, or people with weak digestion, nor, indeed, by any one except in cold weather. Salt pork, bacon, and ham are less objectionable than fresh pork. If fresh pork is desired, obtain it, if possible, from a source where you can be sure the animal has been kept in a cleanly manner and fattened on corn. Fresh pork should be young and firm, the fat white, the lean a pale red, and the skin white and clear. The fat, when salted, should be a delicate pink, and the rind should be thin. Soft, flabby flesh, and yellowish fat with kernels, indicate that the pork is not of the best quality. Unlike other meat, pork is divided into fat and lean. The flank and the thick layer of fat above the flesh are salted. The sides of very young pigs are smoked, as well as salted, and are called bacon. The hams and shoulders are salted and smoked. The head and feet are pickled or boiled, and made into souse or head cheese. After the fat is removed, the loin and ribs are used for roasting or for chops. The lean fat from the kidneys is heated until melted, then strained, cooled, and used as lard. The trimmings of lean and fat, when chopped and highly seasoned, are called sausage meat."[6]

RENT DAY RECIPES

MOCK DUCK
Mrs. L. Alger

In winter, for a large family, buy a shank of beef and have it sawed in three pieces. Cut off as large a piece as possible and have it made into mock duck. Cut a pocket in the meat, fill with dressing and sew up. Sear in spider with a little fat and an onion. Cook like a pot roast for three or four hours. Good either hot or cold. Put the rest of the shank into a large kettle and boil slowly until the meat will drop from the bones. Strain the soup stock, which is very rich, into a bowl for soup. Take the bones out of the meat and put aside the larger pieces of meat. Chop the smaller pieces, and season either with salt, pepper and mustard, or any seasoning you prefer. Pack in a dish or mold with one cup of the soup stock ad put in a cold place to harden. This is very nice for cold meat. The larger pieces of meat can be used for fricassee or meat pie.[12]

AMERICAN CHOP SUEY

1 lb. Hamburg steak
2 onions
½ lb. elbow macaroni

1 tablespoons bacon fat
1 can tomato soup
1 teaspoon salt

Cook macaroni in salted boiling water. Slice onions in bacon fat, and fry until tender. Put onions on side, and fry hamburg steak in remainder of fat with one teaspoon salt. Stir while cooking so it will be brown and crumbly, then add onion and drained macaroni. Pour over this, one can of soup. If in a hurry let the whole boil up once, then serve, but the flavors are better blended if you have time to bake the whole for half an hour in a casserole.[12]

TOAD IN THE HOLE
Mrs. L. Alger

1 lb. hamburg
¼ cup water
6 teaspoons flour
2 eggs
1 pint milk
1 teaspoon salt
1 tablespoon Worcestershire sauce or catsup

Fry one pound hamburg until crumbly. Turn into casserole, and add gravy left in pan to which has been added ¼ cup water. Make batter with six teaspoons flour, 2 eggs, 1 pint milk, 1 teaspoon salt, 1 tablespoon Worcestershire sauce, or catsup, and bake one hour, in moderate oven. This is not a meat pie, but is more like a souffle.[12]

TABLE OF CONTENTS BOOK III MEAT
CONTEMPORARY SOURCES

LINGUICA WITH PEPPERS©
Jennifer Trainer - Great New England Cooks

1½ to 2 pounds sweet or hot linguica
4 to 6 tablespoons water or white wine
3 to 4 tablespoons olive oil
1 large onion, halved and cut into ⅛" slices
4 green or red peppers, or a mixture, stemmed, seeded, and sliced
2 cloves garlic, finely chopped
½ teaspoon dried oregano
salt
freshly ground pepper
2 to 3 teaspoons red wine vinegar

Coil the sausage in a skillet and add the water or wine. Cook over medium heat until the liquid evaporates and the sausage begins to sizzle. Continue to cook, turning the sausage once, until it is browned all over. Remove the sausage and set aside. When the sausage is cool enough to handle, cut it into ½" slices.

Pour the fat from the pan and add the olive oil. Add the onion, peppers, garlic, and oregano and cook, stirring, until the peppers are tender (about ten minutes). Return the sausage to the pan and simmer until heated through. Season with salt, pepper, and vinegar. Serves six.[20]

ROAST PORK AND ORANGE SALAD
Jennifer Trainer - Great New England Cooks©

This main course salad is a good way to use leftover or cold pork. You may choose to cook the pork at home before setting sail or in the cool of the morning once underway to have ready for the evening meal. Cooked beef, chicken, or lamb work well in the recipe, too.

1 pound cold roasted or grilled pork tenderloin, thinly sliced 2 or 3 scallions (white and green parts), thinly sliced 1 red pepper, stemmed seeded, and thinly sliced 3 navel oranges.

Dressing: 1 tablespoon soy sauce 1 teaspoon finely chopped fresh gingerroot 1 clove garlic, finely chopped 1 teaspoon Dijon mustard 1 teaspoon sugar 2 tablespoons white wine or cider vinegar ⅓ cup vegetable oil.

Put the pork in a mixing bowl with the scallions and pepper slices. Combine the dressing ingredients in a container with a tight-fitting lid, shake vigorously and pour over the meat. Toss lightly and set aside to marinate for ten minutes. Using a small, sharp knife cut the peel from the oranges, taking care to remove the white pith. Cut the oranges in half lengthwise and then cut them crosswise into ⅛ inch thick half-moons. Arrange the pork, vegetables, and oranges in overlapping rows on a serving platter. Top with the remaining dressing. Serves 2 to 4.[20]

GREEK LAMB AND BEAN STEW
Elizabeth B. Urmy

2 tablespoons olive oil
1½ pounds lean lamb, diced to walnut size (best cut from the leg)
3 small onions
1 clove garlic, chopped
1 canned tomatoes (drained of juice)

1 canned stock
1½ teaspoon salt
¼ teaspoon fresh ground pepper
½ pound tender green beans slit lengthwise (or frozen Frenched beans)
¼ teaspoon thyme - or better, several sprigs of fresh thyme

Pour olive oil in deep skillet and when hot, brown the lamb chunks, onion and garlic. Add tomatoes, stock and salt and pepper to taste. Let all simmer 1½ to 2 hours, or until lamb is tender. Now add string beans and thyme. When beans are cooked, the stew is ready. Four to six servings.

(Short cut cooks will guess that beans may be fresh or frozen, that four fresh tomatoes or one can of tomato juice and a teaspoon tomato paste may replace tomatoes, and that a bouillon cube will serve for stock. In true Greek manner, the gravy should not be thickened. Tomato juice may be added if necessary.)

SHEPHERD'S PIE
Molly Gordon

1 pound lean ground lamb
2 medium onions diced
1 green or red pepper diced
6 tablespoons of flour
2 cups chicken broth, or red or white wine, or water
Rosemary, thyme, basil, oregano, salt and pepper
2 or 3 large Idaho potatoes, peeled, diced, boiled and mashed with milk and butter, salt and peppered to taste
French fried onions (the kind that come in a can)
Optional: grated mozzarella or Parmesan cheese

Saute the onions and peppers in one or two tablespoons of oil or margerine or butter until limp. Remove to a bowl or a sauce pan. Crumble and brown the lamb, stirring often. Skim off as much fat as possible. Combine lamb, and vegetables and thicken with about 6 tablespoons of flour; stir in liquid to make gravy. Add seasonings, cover and simmer 20 to 30 minutes.

Prepare mashed potatoes, nicely seasoned with enough milk to make them mound prettily. Put lamb and vegetable mix in oven-to-table serving dish and cover with mounds of mashed potato.

Bake at 375° until heated through and nicely browned on top. To add a touch of sinful luxury sprinkle potatoes with grated cheese and run under broiler for a minute. Garnish with French fried onions. This serves four. Recipe is expandable indefinitely.

BEEFSTEAK SMOTHERED IN ONIONS
Fran Vaughan

This recipe comes from THE ORIGINAL PICAYUNE CREOLE COOKBOOK which was first published by The Times Picayune Publishing Company in 1901 in order to ". . . preserve for future generations the many excellent . . . recipes of the New Orleans cuisine by gathering up from the old Creole cooks and the old housekeepers the best of Creole cookery . . ."

3 pounds round steak
1 tbsp. shortening
1 tbsp. flour
2 sprigs each thyme and bay leaf
1 pint water

salt and pepper to taste
6 onions, sliced fine
2 tbsp. vinegar
3 sprigs parsley
1 clove garlic

Beat the Round Steak well with a rolling pin or steak hammer; cut off the outer skin and press the meat back into shape. Place the tablespoon of shortening in the deep frying pan and let it melt. Then lay in the sliced onions, and over these the beefsteak, which has been well seasoned with salt and pepper and dredged with flour. Cover closely. Let it simmer over a hot fire for a few minutes and then turn the steak to the other side. After three minutes add the vinegar, chopped parsley, thyme, bay leaf and garlic. Turn the steak, letting the flour brown well, and keeping the pot closely covered. When brown, pour over one cup of water or a pint, whichever is sufficient to just cover the meat. Bring this to a brisk boil, lower the heat, cover the pot well, and set the pot back where it can simmer gently for about two hours.

When the steak is tender, remove the garlic and bay leaf, put the beefsteak on a platter, and cover with onions and gravy.

TOMATO MEATLOAF
Ann Everest Wojtkowski

1 egg
1 medium onion diced
1 medium green pepper diced
1 can Del Monte "Original Style" stewed tomatoes (14½ oz.)
1 lb. hamburg
2 cups Rice Krispies

In a medium bowl, stir egg until yolk and white are well-mixed. Stir in onion, green pepper, and can of stewed tomatoes. Add hamburg, mixing well. Add Rice Krispies, a handful at a time, coarsely crushing them in the hand before adding to the bowl. Mix thoroughly. If all the liquids have not been absorbed by the Rice Krispies, add more until all liquid has been absorbed. Place mixture in 8" x 8" glass pan. Flatten with bowl or spoon until mixture is same thickness throughout. Bake at 350° for approximately ¾ hour. Serves four to six.

NOTE: Over the years I have modified this recipe from one my mother made that was a favorite. It still is with my family. If you are energy consumption conscious and also want to keep timing simple, place 4 to 6 baking potatoes and 4 to 6 halves of acorn squash in oven at 350°. Then make meatloaf and put in oven. Since the meatloaf only takes about 15 minutes to make, the entire dinner will be ready at the same time.

NEW ENGLAND BEEF SUPPER
Marilyn Avery

2 lbs. lean, tender beef, cut into cubes
2 small onions chopped
1 tablespoon olive oil
1 cup mushrooms quartered
4 medium potatoes, pared, thinly sliced
1 can mushroom soup
¾ cup milk
¾ cup sour cream
½ teaspoon salt
¼ teaspoon pepper
2 cups (or less) shredded cheddar cheese
bread crumbs

Brown meat, onions, and mushrooms in oil in a heavy pan til browned. Add 1 cup water, heat to boiling, then reduce heat and simmer, covered for two hours (add more water or beef broth if necessary). Pour meat into 9 x 13 pan. Arrange potatoes over the meat.

Mix soup, milk, sour cream, salt and pepper. Sprinkle with cheese and top lightly with crumbs. Bake at 350° for about one hour.

CORNISH PASTY
Robert Cooper

¾ lb. top round cut in bite-sized pieces
4 medium potatoes, peeled and chopped
2 medium onions, sliced
2 pie crusts (ready-made?)
salt and pepper to taste

Mix meat, potatoes, onion, salt and pepper in large bowl. Elongate crust slightly, thinning a bit. Place dough on cookie sheet (slightly greased pan). Put ½ of mix on crust, make big "turnover," roll up bottom part of crust and seal with moisture. Prick turnover in several places with fork. Repeat with second crust and rest of mix.

Bake in pre-heated oven at 425° for 45-60 minutes. Dough should brown slightly. Turnover can be frozen. Serves four (can be eaten cold).

RACK OF LAMB WITH ROSEMARY CRUST AND ROSEMARY SAUCE
Keith Emerling

Lamb:
Rack of lamb trimmed of all fat and sinew.
1 bunch of fresh Rosemary (clean, dry, and chopped)
4 to 5 large cloves of garlic, peeled.
Peanut oil

Pat lamb dry with paper towels if needed. Crush garlic and rub it on meat side of rack. Reserve 1 clove and finely chop. Spread Rosemary on counter in a thin layer. Place meat side of rack on herbs until it is completely covered. Generously salt and pepper. Keep uncovered until cooking time.

Sauce:
½ tablespoon unsalted butter
1 medium shallot (chopped fine)
½ cup port wine
1 cup good homemade veal or lamb stock
1½ tablespoon cold unsalted butter
1 dash good port wine

Melt ½ tablespoon of butter in sauce pot. Cook shallot until transparent. Add ¼ cup of port, reserved garlic, 1 tablespoon finely chopped Rosemary, and stock. Cook until reduced and thickened. Keep until serving time.

Equipment:
1 - 10 to 12 inch saute or fry pan
1 - 2 quart sauce pan
1 - oven proof pan
1 - meat thermometer
knives

Place oven proof pan in a 450° preheated oven. Heat saute pan (with a generous coating of peanut oil) until it just begins to smoke. Add rack herb side down. Cook very briefly until lightly browned. Do not burn. Flip and cook until brown. Place in oven proof pan and cook about 8 minutes. Briefly open oven door and reduce heat to 350°. Cook for another 5 to 10 minutes periodically checking with a meat thermometer. For medium rare the meat should be firm to the touch and be about 130-135° in the center. Let rest 3 to 4 minutes.

Bring sauce to a boil. Stir in the cold butter but do not boil. Finish with a splash of good port.

Carve meat vertically between each rib and serve with sauce and your favorite vegetable, potato, and red wine. Serves two people.

COUNTRY RIBS
Barbara Reddington

Place ribs in roasting pan. Cook at 325° for ½ hour. Pour off fat. Cover with a layer of sliced onions. Pour sauce over top; cover. Continue cooking 2½ hours uncovered.

Sauce:
½ cup catsup
¼ teaspoon tabasco
⅛ teaspoon chili powder
½ teaspoon dry mustard
1 tablespoon brown sugar
1 cup water

Double for four or more. Carrots may also be added. Serve with noodles or rice.

PORK TENDERLOIN WITH FRUIT SAUCE
Beverly Trowill

1½ lbs. pork tenderloin
1 8 oz. can pineapple tidbits (in juice)
⅔ cup orange juice
1 tbsp. cornstarch
1 tbsp. soy sauce
¼ tsp. ginger
dash ground red pepper
4 green onions, sliced thin
1 medium carrot, cut into thin strips
1 clove, garlic, minced
1 tbsp. butter or margarine

Roast pork tenderloin in 325° oven, uncovered, for approximately 45 minutes or until thermometer registers 170°. Remove from oven. Cover with foil to keep warm.

Drain pineapple, reserving juice. For sauce, combine reserved juice, orange juice, cornstarch, soy sauce, ginger and red pepper. Set aside.

In large saute pan, cook onions, carrot, and garlic in hot butter or margarine 3 to 4 minutes until crisp-tender. Stir sauce mixture; add to vegetables. Cook and stir until thickened and bubbly, about 2 minutes. Stir in pineapple and heat through. Slice pork; add slices to pineapple mixture until meat is warmed through.

Serve with white rice and a green vegetable. Serves four.

TABLE OF CONTENTS BOOK IV VEGETABLES, SALADS
OLD SOURCES

What plant we in this apple-tree? Fruits that shall swell in sunny June, and redden in the August noon, and drop, when gentle airs come by, That fan the blue September sky, While children come, with cries of glee, And seek them where the fragrant grass, Betrays their bed to those who pass, At the foot of the apple-tree.

WILLIAM CULLEN BRYANT,
PLANTING OF THE APPLETREE

COLD SLAW

Shred a firm cabbage very fine. Mix it with a French dressing, using an extra quantity of salt, or put into a bowl the yolks of three eggs, one half cupful of vinegar (if it is very strong dilute it with water). One tablespoonful butter, one half teaspoonful each mustard and pepper and one teaspoonful each of sugar and salt. Beat them together, place the bowl in pan of boiling water and stir until it becomes a little thickened. Pour this while hot over cabbage and set away to cool.

Robert Sterling Clark, born in 1877, was the grandson of Edward Clark, a major stockholder in the Singer Sewing Machine Company. The wealthy industrialist bred horses, appreciated fine wine and loved art. He and his wife Francine spent a lifetime collecting Degas, Sargents, Renoirs, Monets. Late in his life he became concerned about this magnificent collection. His solution was to build a museum in a place he felt would be safe from nuclear attack. The result was the marble temple known as the Sterling and Francine Clark Art Institute which also was home to the Clarks until his death in 1956.

ROBERT STERLING CLARK'S recipe with comments from his diary.

Dinner - October 20, 1928 - Wonderful eggplant dish. Wonderful eggplant. Mine + Margaret's creation, admirably executed. Parboiled eggplant + mushrooms laid in shallow dish, layer of chopped ham and chicken, sprinkled with grated Parmesan. Put in oven and masked before serving with heavy tomatoes garliced cream sauce.

I never ate a better fancy eggplant dish. It was originally my idea.

Then crisp roasted ducks with wine + liver sauce country fried potatoes + spinach. Ending with crepe suzette, champagne.

3-16-29 In kitchen. Tomato soup too acid. Had Margaret add garlic and I added three tablespoons of current jelly sauce to it! It worked.

When the bean-vines began to flower on the poles, there was one particular variety which bore a vivid scarlet blossom. The daguerreotypist had found these beans in a garret, over one of the seven gables, treasured up in an old chest of drawers, by some horticultural Pyncheon of days gone by, who, doubtless, meant to sow them the next summer, but was himself first sown in Death's garden-ground. By way of testing whether there were still a living germ in such ancient seeds, Holgrave had planted some of them; and the result of his experiment was a splendid row of bean-vines, clambering early, to the full height of the poles, and arraying them, from top to bottom, in a spiral profusion of red blossoms.

NATHANIEL HAWTHORNE,
HOUSE OF SEVEN GABLES

POTATO SALAD

Boil the potatoes with the skins on; when cold remove the skins and cut them into slices three eighths inch thick, or into dice three quarters inch thick, or cut the potatoes into balls with a scoop; sprinkle them with a little grated onion and parsley, chopped very fine. Turn over them a French dressing. They will absorb a great deal. Toss them lightly together, but do not break the potatoes which are very tender. A mayonnaise dressing is also very good with marinated potatoes. A mixture of beets and potatoes with Mayonnaise is also used. Garnish with lettuce, chopped yolk of hard-boiled egg and capers. In boiling potatoes for salad, do not steam them after they are boiled, as they should not be mealy. New or German potatoes are best for salad.[16]

COOKING MUSHROOMS

The simplest way of cooking mushrooms is usually the best, and this may be broiling, sauteeing in butter, or stewing in a little cream sauce. These simple ways may be varied by seasoning with sherry, Madeira, or lemon juice. Any meat stock may be used to stew them in, but many of the mushrooms are very juicy, and their flavor must not be lost by diluting them with too much liquor. They may be cut in pieces when used for sauces. When dried and powdered they make an excellent seasoning for sauces. Dried cepes may be bought at grocers, and are very useful to stew in sauces.

It is better to cook mushrooms as soon as they are peeled, and to rinse them only as much as is necessary, as they lose some flavor by soaking. When they are to be used for garnishing, they are thrown into water with lemon juice, one tablespoonful of juice keeps them, white. The water they are boiled in should be saved to use in sauces. Again they may be put into a saucepan with butter and lemon juice, and cooked (stirring frequently) for about five minutes. They are then covered to keep them white, but the flavor of the mushroom is somewhat destroyed by it, and so it is not recommended for general practice. The French peel the caps with a fluted knife to make them more ornamental, but it is a difficult operation, and does not repay the trouble.[16]

BAKED SQUASH

Choose the Hubbard squash, remove the inside and bake until done, eat with butter like sweet potatoes.[9]

POTATO CROQUETTS
Mrs. W.H. Sperry

Two coffee cupfuls mashed potatoes, one beaten egg; if not moist enough add little cream; season with salt and pepper; roll into balls, then in egg and cracker crumbs and fry in deep fat.[8]

SPRING WONDER
Alice Delleas

Cowslips (without flowers)
Dandelions
Horseradish leaves
Ham or beef bone
Milkweed leaves

It was the habit of our farm family in the spring to go with mother and help gather cowslips (without flowers), dandelions, horseradish leaves and milkweed leaves with tender stems.

Mother would wash and remove the heavy vein in the horseradish, put them all in a kettle with water and a ham bone or bacon and boil until tender. Serve with a sprinkle of cider vinegar. Very good!

MUSHROOMS

Peel the top and stalk, break in small pieces, place them in a stewpan, sprinkle slightly with salt and pepper, and let them stand half an hour, until the juice is drawn out. Stew the mushrooms in the juice and a little butter until tender, add cream to cover, and when the cream is hot serve on toast. Mushrooms are considered difficult of digestion. They are a fungus growth, and have a woody odor and a meaty flavor. They are used largely in sauces. Unless familiar with the difference between the edible and the poisonous mushrooms, it is safer to use the canned mushrooms, or to obtain the fresh at a reliable market.[6]

CAULIFLOWER

Boil it in water for one hour and then add two cups of milk and boil for another hour, gently. Put into a deep dish and turn over it drawn butter.[9]

ASPARAGUS

Cut up the green ends and chop up the remainder of the stalks; boil them until tender, and season with salt and pepper; have ready some toasted bread in a deep dish; mix together equal parts of flour and butter to a cream; add to this slowly enough of the asparagus water or clear hot water to make a sauce; boil up once; put the asparagus on the toast and pour over the sauce.[9]

TO COOK SQUASH AND PUMPKIN

Wash clean, take out inside, cut up without paring, put into steamer and steam. When done, sift through colander. Steaming makes it drier and more mealy, and leaving the skin on renders it sweeter. In sifting, the skin remains in the colander.[9]

If boiling water is poured over oranges before peeling, the white skin will come off with the peeling and will give the oranges a better flavor.[3]

When a large quantity of potatoes must be cooked, add the juice of a lemon to the boiling water and the potatoes will be snowy white.[12]

DANDELION SALAD

Dandelions and lettuce, cold boiled potatoes and hard boiled eggs, and a little onion chopped fine, ordinary salad dressing without mustard.[9]

HOT SLAW

Place shredded cabbage in a saucepan with enough salted boiling water to cover it. Boil it until tender, but not so long as to lose shape; turn it onto a sieve and drain it well in a warm place. Pour over the drained cabbage a hot Bearnaise sauce.

Cabbage salads are good to serve with fried oysters, meat fritters, or chops.

The boiled cabbage, cold, may be used with French dressing.[16]

CABBAGE SALAD

One head cabbage chopped fine, one dozen eggs boiled hard and chopped. Make a dressing of one quart vinegar, half cup butter, half cup vinegar (sic), a third cup of mustard. Salt and pepper, scald, and while hot pour over cabbage and eggs. This will keep.[9]

CORN PUDDING

Scrape with a knife two dozen ears of green corn, cutting each row through the middle. Add one pint of milk, half a pound of butter, three eggs, the whites and yolks beaten separately, a little salt, and white pepper. Stir the yolks into the milk and corn, pour into a baking-dish, stir in the whites, and bake an hour and a half.[16]

SUCCOTASH

Cut the corn from the cobs and put in one-third beans and boil in water enough to cover until tender. Then season with pepper, salt, and a little milk; simmer together a few moments and serve.[9]

SCALLOPED TOMATOES

Scald and peel half a dozen tomatoes, set them in a buttered dish, sprinkle with pepper, salt and a dust of powdered sugar; cover with buttered dry crumbs and bake till brown.[8]

STUFFED TOMATOES

Cut a thin slice off the tops of eight large firm tomatoes and with a spoon carefully lift out the pulp, rub it through a sieve discarding the seeds. To the juice add half a cup of stale bread crumbs, two tablespoonfuls of melted butter, a dust of salt, pepper and paprika and half a teaspoonful of minced parsley. Stuff the tomato shells with this, put a bit of butter on top of each and set in a hot oven for ten minutes.[8]

CAULIFLOWER AU GRATIN

Boil the cauliflower. Melt a tablespoonful of butter in a saucepan and stir smoothly in one tablespoonful of flour, thin with half a pint of milk, stir until boiling; add flour, tablespoonfuls of grated cheese and salt to taste and dash of cayenne. Pour this over the cauliflower and serve hot.[8]

When making cranberry sauce cut the cranberries in two, put in a bowl of cold water over night. In the morning you will find that the seeds have all sunk to the bottom. Skim off the berries and proceed as usual. [12]

When separating seeded raisins, wet your fingers in cold water first and the raisins will not stick to you. [12]

BAKED TOMATOES

Pare and slice, cover the bottom of a dish with bread crumbs or crackers, put in a layer of tomatoes and sprinkle crumbs over them; fill up the dish with crumbs for last layer; season the whole with salt and pepper.[9]

TOMATO HASH

Butter the dish well; put in a layer of sliced tomatoes, a layer of cold meat, sliced thin; then a layer of bread and butter, and so on until the dish is full, seasoning well with pepper and salt, and beaten eggs poured over the top. Bake brown.[9]

ONION PIE

Take a deep dish and insert a small cup in the center. Place in the bottom of layer of sliced meat, one of potatoes, and one of onions. Season with salt and pepper; then another layer of meat, potatoes and onions, and continue until the dish is full; then fill up center with cold water, cover and set in the stove; and cook until half an hour before it is wanted. Make a rich pie crust and put it over the top and set in the oven to bake.[9]

VEGETABLE HASH
Mrs. Apollos Root

Take whatever remains of the meat, beets, carrots, turnips and potatoes after a boiled dinner, chop fine, pour into a pan in which a slice of pork has been fried, cover and brown.[12]

TABLE OF CONTENTS BOOK IV
VEGETABLES / SALADS CONTEMPORARY SOURCES

APPETIZER OR SALAD LORENZO
Marge Champion

1 ripe fresh papaya
1 bunch watercress
¾ pound small bay shrimp
1 bottle Heinz or Country Chili Sauce
1 tablespoon olive oil
Sherry wine vinegar to taste or wine vinegar with 1½ teaspoons
  sherry wine added
Lettuce leaves and watercress garnish

Chop watercress (minus stems) quite fine. Peel and slice papaya and arrange on bed of lettuce leaves with sprigs of watercress. Mix chili sauce, olive oil, wine vinegar, and chopped watercress. (Use about two cups of sauce.) Heap cooked bay shrimp on lettuce bed. (Use 2 or 3 tablespoons of shrimp each serving if preparing individual servings.) Place generous helping of sauce on top.

SERVE AND RECEIVE COMPLIMENTS! BROCCOLI SALAD
Beverly Trowill

1 large head broccoli (floweretts only)
8 - 10 slices bacon, cooked crisp and broken into pieces
1 carrot grated
½ cup cheddar cheese, shredded

Dressing:
1 cup mayonnaise
2 tbsp. cider vinegar
⅓ cup sugar

Mix dressing ingredients together until well mixed. Toss dressing with broccoli, bacon, carrot and cheese. Prepare several hours before serving and keep refrigerated. Serves four.

FROZEN PEA SALAD
Audrey Sweeney

Colorful and popular on a buffet table.

2 pks. frozen peas, thawed but not cooked
2 cups chopped celery
½ cup chopped green onions (scallions)

½ pint sour cream
Salt, pepper, seasoning salt to taste.

These ingredients may be mixed ahead and refrigerated. Just before serving add:

½ cup salted cashews, chopped
12 (or less) slices bacon, cooked very crisp and crumbled.

Serves eight. Salt, pepper, seasoning salt to taste.

WHITE-WHITE CHICKEN SALAD
Winnie Neveu

First mixture: In wooden chopping bowl dice 2 cups cooked chicken breast. Toss lightly with ¼ cup diced green pepper, 1 scallion sliced diagonally, and ½ cup celery (white stalks, not green), sliced thinly and diagonally. Refrigerate while preparing the following.

Second mixture: ¼ cup heavy cream whipped stiff to which add ½ teaspoon chicken bouillon granules and a sprinkling of white pepper. Add salt only if you think it needs it.

Combine above two mixtures and serve very cold. Garnish with your imagination!

CHINESE CHICKEN SALAD
Winnie Neveu

Comment: "The Chinese never heard of this salad because it originated in my Cheshire kitchen."

Cooked chicken sliced in small long pieces. Thinly sliced celery and a few leaves chopped as well, for flavor. Fresh, raw peas (do not include pods) or frozen, uncooked peas (drained) or—if you get desperate—canned, drained peas. Soy sauce, about a tablespoonful. Salt and pepper, Chow mein crispy noodles and mayonnaise.

Combine any amounts of the above ingredients to suit your taste. Serve immediately.

CUCUMBER MOUSSE
Robert Cooper

1 package (3 ounce) lime jello
1 cup boiling water
1 tablespoon vinegar
1 tablespoon grated onion

1 cup finely chopped cucumber (approximately 1½ cukes)
1 cup sour cream or yogurt
¼ cup mayonnaise

Stir jello in boiling water until dissolved. Add vinegar and onion and refrigerate until syrupy.

Beat in sour cream/yogurt, mayonnaise and well-drained cucumber. Pour into mold (or 4 individual molds) and refrigerate until set.

Note: Can use quick blender to chop cucumbers—drain and squeeze through cheesecloth.

FRESH RASPBERRY SPINACH SALAD
Anne Everest Wojtkowski

1 pint of fresh raspberries (or strawberries)
Fresh spinach for four salads
6 oz. fresh, white, button mushrooms, cleaned and sliced
¼ cup raspberry (or strawberry) syrup
¼ cup Italian dressing

Thoroughly wash and drain (spin dry, if you have such a wonderful device) enough spinach to nearly fill four salad bowls. Proportionately distribute berries and mushrooms onto tops of each bed of spinach. Pour syrup and dressing into a container with a secure top, and shake vigorously. Pour over salad just before serving. Serves four.

NOTE: There have been times when I planned to serve this salad and purchased all the ingredients thinking that I had the syrup on hand, only to discover I didn't. On those occasions, I spooned raspberry or strawberry jelly into a small pot and added enough water to thin it to the consistency of a syrup and warmed it up, mixing constantly, to produce essentially the same ingredient.

SPINACH AND RICE RING
Kitty Lichtenstein

2 packages frozen chopped spinach, cooked
¾ cup milk
2 whole eggs, lightly beaten
1½ cups cooked brown rice
1 small onion, grated
Dash of nutmeg (optional)
Seasoning to taste

Mix all ingredients together, adding milk and beaten eggs last. Bake in 400° oven for 30 minutes. Serves four.

SIMMERED CARROTS
Barbara Reddington

12 carrots
½ cup sugar
¼ cup oil
1 onion, diced
1 tablespoon Worcestershire sauce
1 can tomato soup
¼ cup vinegar
1 tablespoon mustard
1 red pepper

Cook the carrots. Set aside. Simmer about 15 minutes. Pour remaining ingredients over carrots.

ZUCCHINI CASSEROLE
Robert Cooper

1 lb. zucchini (3 small/medium)
2 tablespoons butter or margarine
3 garlic cloves
1 medium onion, sliced
1 green pepper, sliced
2 cups canned, peeled tomatoes (14 - 16 oz.)
1 teaspoon salt
⅛ teaspoon pepper
¼ teaspoon oregano
small package shredded cheddar cheese
1 cup dried bread crumbs (2 to 3 slices cut in squares)

Cut washed zucchini into ¼" discs. Put in greased casserole dish. Melt butter in skillet. Add peppers, onions, garlic. Cook until onion is transparent; add salt, pepper, oregano and tomatoes to skillet. Bring to a boil. Remove garlic cloves and toss away. Pour rest of skillet over zucchini and mix gently.

Place covered casserole in pre-heated oven at 350°. Cook until zucchini is nearly tender (35 - 40 minutes). Remove casserole from oven, sprinkle with crumbs and cheese. Bake uncovered for fifteen minutes more.

SUMMER SQUASH CASSEROLE
Lee Leahy Stanfield

From *The Eagle*, September 25, 1989 with this personal comment: "I can attest to the popularity of this. I have made it often since Betty Jane first introduced me to it on my front porch, and it is always a hit!"

6 cups summer squash
¼ cup chopped onion
1 can cream of celery soup
1 pkg. (7 or 8 oz.) Pepperidge Farm herb stuffing mix

1 cup sour cream
1 cup grated carrot
1 stick margarine

Cook squash and onion in salted water. Drain. Add sour cream, grated carrot and celery soup. Melt margarine and combine with stuffing mix. Layer a large casserole with stuffing, squash mix, and stuffing. Bake at 350° for 30 minutes.

ASPARAGUS WITH LEMON BUTTER
Carolyn E. Banfield

2 lbs. fresh asparagus (or 2, 10 ounce pkgs. frozen asparagus cuts)
½ teaspoon salt

¼ cup soft butter or margarine
2 teaspoons lemon juice

Break off tough ends of asparagus stalks. Wash tips well with cold water. With vegetable parer, scrape skin and scales from lower part of stalk only. With sharp knife, cut stalks on the diagonal, making bias slices about 1 inch long. In medium skillet with tight-fitting cover, bring ⅓ cup water to boiling. Add asparagus and salt: cook, covered and over high heat, 5 to 8 minutes. Drain. Add butter and lemon juice, tossing until butter is melted.

AVOCADOS: For Goodness's Sake!
Mary H. Bardwell

Avocados are in season most of the year. Personally, I prefer California ones as they have a richer flavor. The following is for an avocado ring. This is great if one is not on a diet.

Dissolve two pkgs. gelatin in 1½ cups hot water and let cool. Then fold in 1½ cups mayonnaise, juice of half a lemon, 2 pureed avocados and ½ pint of whipped cream.

Chill until firm in a ring mold and fill center with crab, tomatoes or shredded lettuce and French dressing.

CAULIFLOWER WITH LEMON BUTTER
Carolyn E. Banfield

2 heads cauliflower (1¾ lbs. each)
½ cup butter or margarine, melted
⅔ cup lemon juice
6 tablespoons bottled capers, drained
2 tablespoons chopped parsley
2 tablespoons chopped chives (optional)

Wash cauliflower thoroughly, and cut into flowerets. Cook, covered, in 1" lightly salted boiling water for about 10 minutes, until tender. Drain well. Meanwhile, combine butter, lemon juice, and capers. Turn cauliflower into serving dish; pour heated lemon butter over the top. Sprinkle with parsley and chives.

SWEET POTATO CRUNCH
Helen Plunkett

1 can (1 lb. sweet potatoes)

Topping:
¼ cup butter or margarine, melted
½ cup light-brown sugar, firmly packed
½ cup corn flakes

Preheat oven to 400°. Grease a seven or eight inch pie plate. Drain potatoes, reserving ½ cup liquid. Mash potatoes. Gradually add reserved liquid, stirring until well combined. Turn into prepared pie plate, spreading evenly. Make topping: Toss butter, sugar and corn flakes to combine. Sprinkle evenly over potatoes. Bake, uncovered, 20 minutes, or until topping is golden-brown and crispy. Makes four servings.

TABLE OF CONTENTS   BOOK V COOKIES / CAKES / PIES OLD SOURCES

After the more solid portion of the banquet had been duly honored, the cakes and sweet preparations of various kinds began to get their share of attention. There were great cakes and little cakes, cakes with raisins in them, cakes with currants, and cakes without either. There were brown cakes and yellow cakes, frosted cakes, glazed cakes, hearts and rounds and "jumbles" which playful youth slip over the forefinger before spoiling their annular outline.

OLIVER WENDELL HOLMES,
ELSIE VENNER

SOFT GINGER COOKIES
Frances Melville Thomas
½ cup sugar
⅓ cup lard
⅓ cup butter (use full amount of shortening or bacon fat)
1 egg

Take ½ cup molasses; into it put 1¼ tsp. soda and set in bowl to foam 5 minutes.

Cream sugar and shortening. Beat egg lightly; add to sugar and shortening, add molasses and stir; add 2 tbs. cold water and 1 tbs. vinegar, 3 cups sifted pastry flour, with ½ tsp. ginger and ½ tsp. salt. Drop from spoon onto cookie sheet. Do not overbake as this will make them hard.

THESE COOKIES WERE MADE BY THE COOK IN THE HOUSEHOLD OF FRANCES MELVILLE THOMAS, HERMAN MELVILLE'S DAUGHTER, AND MELVILLE CHAPIN'S GRANDMOTHER.

SPONGE CAKE

Ten eggs, the weight of the eggs in sugar, the weight of five eggs in flour, grated peel and juice of a lemon. Beat the yolks and sugar together till white and creamy, whip the whites to a stiff froth, put together and stir in flour lightly, adding lemon last. This receipt has been used for several generations in one family and is much prized.[1]

The country-girl, willing to give her utmost assistance, proposed to make an Indian cake, after her mother's peculiar method, of easy manufacture, and which she could vouch for as possessing a richness, and, if rightly prepared, a delicacy, unequaled by another mode or breakfast-cake. Hepzibah gladly assenting, the kitchen was soon the scene of savory preparation.

NATHANIEL HAWTHORNE,
HOUSE OF SEVEN GABLES

BUTTER COOKIES - Mrs. William Cullen Bryant
From her recipe book of 1831

This recipe has been tried and updated by Colette Christian, chef at the Ashfield Inn.

3 cups flour
¾ teaspoon baking soda
½ teaspoon salt 1 cup sugar
2 sticks butter, unsalted
2 eggs
1½ teaspoons vanilla extract

Sift together flour, baking soda, salt—set aside. Cream butter until fluffy and light in color. Gradually add sugar and combine well. Add eggs one at a time. Add vanilla extract. Add flour. Mix until combined. Roll mixture into a log or roll. Wrap in foil. Refrigerate at least 1 hour. Cut into ¼ inch slices. Brush with milk and sprinkle with granulated sugar. Bake at 350° for eight to ten minutes.

FRUIT CAKE, 1848
From "Esther," a friend of Mrs. William Cullen Bryant,
Mrs. Bryant's recipe book.

½ lb flour
½ lb. sugar
½ lb. raisins
1 oz. of mace
½ gill of brandy
½ lb of butter
½ lb of currants
½ lb of Citron
3 nut megs
6 eggs

Rub the butter and sugar together. 1 teaspoonful of saleratus and 1 teacupful of molasses. The more you beat it the better. This will make three cakes. Bake it one hour and a half.

THESE RECIPES CAME FROM THE COOKBOOK OF MRS. WILLIAM CULLEN BRYANT. BRYANT WAS A TRUE BERKSHIREITE HAVING BEEN BORN IN CUMMINGTON AND HAVING PRACTICED LAW IN GREAT BARRINGTON.

MARSH RECIPES
John Hyde's Family Cookbook

This handwritten "receipt" account signed by Mrs. George Marsh. May 8, 1858

TEMPERANCE CAKE

¼ cup butter
1 cup chopped raisins
2½ cups of flour
1 cup sugar
1 cup sour milk
teaspoon saleratus (A common name for baking soda long ago.)
spice

TUMBLER CAKE

1 tumbler of butter
2 tumblers sugar
3 tumblers flour
1 tumbler milk
1 teaspoon saleratus
2 teaspoons cream of tartar
4 eggs

HOLLOWELL CAKE

2 cups butter
3 cups sugar
5 cups flour
3 cups raisins
1 cup milk
5 eggs
1 glass brandy
2 teaspoons cream of tartar
1 teaspoon soda
1 teaspoon cloves
1 teaspoon cinnamon

APPLE CUSTARD FOR PIES

4 pounds strained apples
1 pound sugar
1 pound melted butter
1 pint cream
7 eggs spice lemon[5]

GINGER SNAPS

Mrs. Ely

2 cups boiled molasses
1 cup shortening
large teaspoon saleratus
ginger
cinnamon [5]

INDIAN JOHNNY CAKE

1½ Indian meal
1 cup flour
1 cup sour milk
1 egg
a little saleratus*
2 tablespoons molasses

*Note: Saleratus - sodium bicarbonate (baking soda) [5]

MOUNTAIN CAKE

1 cup white sugar
whites of 2 eggs
½ cup butter
½ cup milk
2 cups flour
1 teaspoon cream of tartar
½ teaspoon soda
vanilla [5]

PORK CAKE

¾ pound salt pork chopped fine
1 pint milk poured on the pork boiling hot
1½ cups sugar
1½ cup molasses
2 eggs
1 pound raisins
cloves, cinnamon, nutmeg
1 teaspoon soda
4½ cups flour [5]

SHAKER CHOCOLATE POUND CAKE

Lawrence J. Yerdon, Director
Hancock Shaker Village, Inc.   Pittsfield, MA

Recipe from the original found at Hancock Shaker Village and included in *Best of Shaker Cooking*, Miller and Fuller.

1 cup butter	3 cups sifted flour
5 eggs	¼ teaspoon vanilla
½ teaspoon baking powder	3 cups sugar
2 tablespoons grated chocolate	½ cup cocoa
½ cup lard	1¼ cup milk

Cream butter, shortening, and sugar together until light and fluffy. Add eggs, one at a time, beating well after each addition. Sift together flour, cocoa, baking powder, and salt; add alternately with milk to egg mixture, stirring after each addition until well blended. Add chocolate. Stir in vanilla.

Turn batter into greased and floured tube-type or loaf pan. Bake in preheated 325° oven for 1½ hours. Turn onto wire rack to cool. Serve with whipped cream or ice cream.

In buying cake pans, buy two alike and use one for the cover when wrapping a cake that has soft frosting.[1]

Add one tablespoon of vinegar to the cake batter and the cake will not fall. It will not affect the flavor of the cake.[9]

PAN DOWDY

Cover a deep pie plate with crust. Put in a layer of sliced apple, then thin shavings of salt pork, then more apple, and more pork. Bake with an upper crust. When done take off the upper crust and turn it over on a plate. Season the apple with sugar, molasses and allspice. Put half the apple on the upper crust, then lay this on the half and serve hot.[1]

HASTY PUDDING

Put on water according to the size of your family. Sift five or six spoonfuls of meal into a bowl of water, and when the kettle boils, stir it in and let it boil up thick. Then stand over the kettle and sprinkle in meal, handful after handful, stirring it thoroughly all the time. When it is so thick the pudding stick stands up in it, it is about right. Cook half an hour. Eat it with milk or molasses. Either Indian meal or rye meal may be used. Rye hasty pudding and West Indian molasses as a diet, would save many a one the dyspepsia.[1]

BLOCK CHOCOLATE CAKE
Mrs. E.I. Fessenden

Two cakes of grated chocolate, one cup of brown sugar, one yolk, one-half cup of milk, cook until it thickens. For cake, one cup of brown sugar, one egg, one-half cup of butter, two-thirds cup of milk, one cup of flour. Stir this, add the chocolate when cold, also one cup of flour, one teaspoonful of soda, bake in layers, put together with boiled white frosting.[2]

PORK APPLE PIE

Line a deep plate with crust, put in a layer of apples and pieces of pork cut very thin, until the plate is very full, sugar, allspice and pepper. Put on top crust and bake slow for one hour; to be eaten warm.[9]

MORE MARSH RECIPES

A new kind of cake "Patented August 1871"

EDWARDS PINK CAKE

1 cup butter
2 eggs
4 cups flour
1 cup molasses

Roll thin. Beat in the whites of two eggs. Keep till cold. Spread molasses on top. Eat when convenient.[5]

DOG CAKE

¾ cup flour
2 eggs
1 tablespoon salt
1 teaspoon rice

Bake until done. Serve up on a platter.[5]

BLACK FRUITCAKE

2 pounds raisins
2 pounds currants
½ pound citron
1½ pounds butter
1 nutmeg
1 wineglass brandy
1 pound sugar
1 pound flour
2 eggs[5]

Add a tablespoonful of minute tapioca to the filling of a fruit pie, it helps retain the juice and improves the consistency.[12]

A little lemon juice added to pastry dough will make it much lighter.[3]

PIES

At some seasons of the year, fresh pie timber runs short. Make a good deal of rich mince meat in the fall. With occasional scalding it may be kept nearly the year round. A bushel of dried apples helps fill the gap. Boil and sift pumpkin, spread it on tin plates, and dry hard in a warm oven. When wanted for use soak it in milk. Carrot grated and cooked like squash makes delicious pies. Dried huckleberries are very good. A pie of boiled raisins chopped, with a rolled cracker stirred in requires very little extra seasoning and is not expensive. A little ingenuity added to almost any material that comes to hand, will make a tasty pie. If all things fail, puddings must be substituted, but they do not take the place.

At Thanksgiving time it saves labor to make seventy-five or a hundred pies, and keep them on hand. Freeze them and slip the covered ones from the plates. Pack them in an earthen crock or large chest, one upon another, and thaw as needed.[16]

PIES AND PUFF-PASTE

The American pie is perhaps the most ridiculed of all dishes. It has, however, great popularity and undoubted merits. Were the crust, especially the under one, always right, it would remove the most salient point of criticism. The tart pies, made with puff-paste, are a temptation to the most fastidious taste. The mince pie, probably the most indigestible of all, is the one universally accepted as a treat, and seldom refused by the scoffer. Pies have their seasons, like other good things, the apple pie being the only one served the year round. The berries and fruits, each one in their time, make most acceptable and delicious pies and tarts, while rhubarb introduces the spring, and pumpkin announces the autumn. In this day of canned and dried fruits the season need not be so strictly observed, but fresh fruits will always be preferable to preserved ones, and tradition goes far to hold the place for pumpkin pie at Thanksgiving, and mince pie at the Christmas feasts.[16]

MAPLE SUGAR PIE

Line plate with crust, making a raised edge; cut your sugar in small lumps and place two inches apart over the paste, in between put bits of butter. Take one egg, one teaspoon of flour, one large cup of milk, allspice, cover and bake slow.[9]

TEMPERANCE MINCE PIES

One and one-half pints of chopped meat, three pints chopped apples, one-half pint each of vinegar and fruit syrup, two pints of sugar, one pint raisins, two tablespoonfuls of cinnamon and a grated nutmeg. Before putting on top crust, drop in bits of butter.[15]

CAKE

The production of good cake requires particular care and every careful housewife will take pains to perfect herself in this necessary art. Every well-regulated family will keep a sufficient quantity of rich fruit cake on hand for chance visitors or other occasions. This can be made before Thanksgiving, of a richness to ensure its keeping six or even twelve months. Should it become moldy on the outside the mold can be removed with a damp cloth and the cake set in a hot oven for a few moments when it will become as good as new.

Gingerbread, seedcakes, and doughnuts will suffice for daily needs. In all cases where spices are named it is supposed they be pounded fine and sifted, sugar must be dried and rolled fine, flour dried in an oven, eggs well beat or whipped to a raging foam. Pearlash is a necessary ingredient in all cakes made with sour or butter-milk. Thrifty housekeepers are wont to gather the whitest and lightest of applewood ashes as they fall in the fireplace. These should be leached with water and put into bottles.

A manufactured article called soda is used in conjunction with cream of tartar and sweet milk to make light delicious cakes.[1]

Put a teaspoon of vinegar in the fat in which doughnuts are fried. It makes them lighter and they brown evenly.[12]

A dessertspoon of vinegar added to a cup of milk will help you make as light as you ever tasted. Equals two eggs.[3]

SCRIPTURE

One cup of butter, Judges 5:25; three and one-half cups flour, First Kings 4:22; two cups sugar, Jeremiah 6:20; two cups raisins, First Samuel 30:12; two cups figs, First Samuel 30:12: one cup water, Genesis 24:17; one cup almonds, Genesis 43:11; six eggs, Isaiah 10:14; one tablespoonful honey, Exodus 16:31; a pinch of salt, Leviticus 2:13; spice to taste, First Kings 10:10. Follow Solomon's advice for making good boys and you will have a good cake, Prov. 23:14.[15]

WHORTLEBERRY CAKE

Three pints flour, one cup sugar, one-half cup of butter, two teaspoons cream of tartar, one of soda, one pint of milk, a pinch of salt, and one pint of berries. Bake three-quarters of an hour.[9]

FRUIT CAKE

One pound of butter, one of sugar, one of flour, two of raisins, two of currants, one-quarter of a pound of citron, ten eggs, half a cup of molasses, one teaspoon of soda dissolved in two tablespoons of sour milk, half a gill of brandy, and spices of all kinds to taste.[9]

MOLASSES COOKIES

One pint of molasses, one coffee cup of butter and lard, boil ten minutes, when nearly cool, add three tablespoonfuls of boiling water, one tablespoonful of soda, stir until it foams, then add a little salt, one tablespoonful of ginger, mix very soft with flour, good, try them.[2]

JUMBLES

One teacup pulverized sugar, one teacup of butter, three teacups of flour, three eggs. Sprinkle the table with powdered sugar, break off pieces of the dough and roll in the sugar, and then wind or tie them in any shape you wish.[9]

MADELEINES No. 2

Take a sponge-cake No. 1 or a Genoese cake mixture, and make it a little stiffer with flour (enough batter can usually be saved from layer cake to make a few fancy cakes). With a spoon or pastry-bag drop it in balls one half inch in diameter; bake, and place two together with a little jam or jelly between them. Cover them with soft royal icing; have them all the same color. If green, use pistachio flavor, and sprinkle the tops with chopped pistachio nuts; if white, with almonds; if pink, leave them plain, and flavor with rose.[16]

LADIES FINGERS
Mrs. H.C. Wells

One cup of sugar, one-half cup of butter, beat together, one egg, one-fourth cup of milk, one pint of flour, one teaspoonful of cream of tartar, one-half teaspoonful of soda, one teaspoonful of vanilla, cut into little strips, roll in sugar, bake in quick oven, use your hands to roll them instead of a rolling pin.[2]

MOCK MINCE PIES — delicious

Eighteen Boston crackers rolled fine, two cups sugar, one of molasses, one cup sharp vinegar, one-half cup of water, one wine glass of brandy, one cup and a half of raisins, one-fourth pound of citron, one tablespoon of each of cinnamon, cloves and nutmeg, a piece of butter the size of an egg, melted and stirred in, and a little salt.[9]

RECIPES FROM TOR COURT

Pat Schively

During the years we lived at Tor Court (1928 - 1933), Sophie Swenson was the cook for the Salisburys. My Mother had the following two recipes in her box, the cards are brown with age and the corners of the 3 x 5 cards are rounded off. We often had the Muffin recipe, and I and my children still make Sophie's Muffins frequently, so we know the recipe works. I remember eating her Sugar Cookies but have never tried to make them myself. The cookies were thin and crisp. I don't know if the instructions are detailed enough for today's cooks, but submit them as they were given to Mother. *(See also page 55).*

SUGAR COOKIES

1 cup soft butter
1 cup sugar
Vanilla or lemon flavoring
4 eggs, slightly beaten

2 tbsp. cold water
5 large cups flour
2 tsp. baking powder

Put in ice box to set. Roll very thin. Bake 5 minutes or so in hot oven.

SOPHIE'S PLAIN MUFFINS

1 large spoon butter
½ cup sugar
1 egg

½ cup milk
1 cup flour
1 heaping tsp. baking powder

Makes quickly. Bake in hot oven 6 to 10 minutes. Makes 12.

(N.B. I set oven at 400°. Texture is not right if they bake more than ten minutes. (Chopped pecans or blueberries can also be added.)

TABLE OF CONTENTS   BOOK V COOKIES / CAKES / PIES CONTEMPORARY SOURCES

THE PERFECT DOUBLE CHOCOLATE CHIP COOKIES
GRANDPRIZE DOUBLE CHOCOLATE CHIP COOKIES

Gwen Steege

The grand prize-winning recipe of all 2600 submitted to The Orchards' contest in 1987 is this rich, moist, double chocolate cookie. The cookies were judged by three editors from Chocolatier, Orchards pastry chef Heather Andrus, and owners of the inn, Chester and Carol Soling. Each judge had three minutes to savor each cookie and rank it on a scale of one to ten. Sips of cold milk, water, or champagne cleared their palates for the next tasting.

1¾ cups flour	1 cup granulated sugar	⅓ cup unsweetened cocoa
¼ teaspoon baking soda	½ cup dark brown sugar, firmly packed	2 tablespoons milk
1 cup butter of margarine, softened	1 egg	1 cup chopped pecans or walnuts
1 teaspoon vanilla extract		

Combine flour and baking soda, and set aside. Use an electric mixer to cream butter. Add vanilla and sugars, and beat until fluffy. Beat in egg. At low speed beat in cocoa, then milk. With a wooden spoon mix in dry ingredients just until blended. Stir in nuts and chocolate chips.

Drop by rounded teaspoonfuls onto nonstick or foil-lined baking sheets. Bake at 350° for 12 to 13 minutes. Remove from oven and cool slightly before removing from baking sheets. Yield: 3 dozen. This recipe was first published in Winning at the Table by the Junior League of Las Vegas.

PEANUT BUTTER-CHOCOLATE CHIP COOKIES

Dan Lee

1 cup shortening	1 teaspoon vanilla	2 teaspoons baking soda
1 cup granulated sugar	1 cup peanut butter (creamy or chunky)	½ teaspoon salt
1 cup packed brown sugar	2 cups sifted all-purpose flour	Chocolate chips (whatever amount you like)
2 eggs		

Thoroughly cream shortening, sugars, eggs, and vanilla. Stir in peanut butter. Sift dry ingredients; stir into creamed mixture. Add chocolate chip (the bigger the better!) Drop by rounded teaspoons onto ungreased cookie sheet. Bake at 350° for about 10 minutes. Makes about 5 dozen cookies.

From the HOME COMFORT COOK BOOK:

LADY FINGERS

1 cup sugar
1 egg
½ cup butter
¼ cup milk
½ tsp. soda
1 pint flour
1 tsp. cream of tartar
1¼ tsp. vanilla

Cut in strips, roll in sugar and bake in quick oven.

From MRS. BLAKE'S RADIO COLUMN:

DROP COOKIES

1 cup Crisco
½ cup sugar
3 eggs
3½ cups flour
2½ tsp. baking powder
¾ cup milk
½ tsp. salt
1 tsp. cinnamon
¼ tsp. cloves
1 cup chopped nuts
1 cup seedless raisins

Blend Crisco, sugar and eggs. Sift dry ingredients, combine with Crisco mixture and milk. Blend well. Drop by teaspoonfuls on cookie sheet and bake in a moderate oven, about 375°. About 12 minutes.

CRANBERRY PECAN BARS
Shirley S. Clute

For crust:
½ cup softened butter
2 teaspoons vanilla
2 tablespoons sugar
½ teaspoon salt
1 cup flour
½ cup finely chopped pecans

For topping:
2 cups chopped cranberries
½ cup flaked coconut
½ cup finely chopped pecans
2 tablespoons flour
grated rind of one orange
2 cups sugar
3 egg yolks
⅓ cup cream

To make crust: Mix butter and vanilla with sugar, salt, and flour, mixing until crumbly. Stir in chopped pecans. Press mixture in a very thin layer in a greased 9 x 13 inch pan. Bake at 350° for about 10 minutes, or until lightly brown.

Meanwhile: Mix together the chopped cranberries, coconut, chopped pecans, flour, grated orange rind, sugar, egg yolks, and cream. Pour over crust and bake 30 to 40 minutes. Cut into bars and remove from pan immediately upon removal from oven.

COWBOY COOKIES
Audrey Sweeney

The favorite of my boys, no matter what their age; sent to them all over the world!

Cream together:
1 cup shortening
1 cup sugar
1 cup brown sugar

2 eggs, beaten (Make a "well" in above ingredients and beat eggs in the well.)

Sift and add:
2 cups sifted flour
1 tsp. soda
½ tsp. salt
½ tsp. baking powder

1 tsp. vanilla
2 cups Quick Quaker Oats
Semi-sweet chocolate bits, 6 or 12 ounces
Raisins and nuts if desired.

Ungreased cookie sheet, 12 to 15 minutes, 350° oven. (Drop by teaspoon, 20 on sheet, makes 70 cookies.)

EASY PEANUT BUTTER/PEANUT BUTTER CHOCOLATE CHIP COOKIES
Norma J. Zullo

1 can condensed milk
¾ cup peanut butter
2 cups Bisquick

1 teaspoon vanilla
1 small package chocolate bits

Mix condensed milk and peanut butter together. Add Bisquick and vanilla; mix well. Form into balls.

For just peanut butter cookies, flatten both ways with a fork.

For chocolate chips, mix bits with batter and leave ball shape.

Bake in 350° oven for only 3 or 4 minutes or until light brown on bottom.

PINEAPPLE COOKIES
Lee Stanfield

My favorite cookie recipe is for Pineapple Cookies, which have appeared in *The Eagle* a couple of times over the years. Mazie Riddle made these to take on a trip to Vermont with the children when they were small, must have been about 50 years ago. I made these for a party at the YMCA pool when I reached the 1,000-mile mark.

Cream together:
2/3 cup shortening
1 1/3 cups sugar
2 eggs
2 teaspoons lemon extract

Add and mix together:
2 1/3 cups flour
1/2 teaspoon baking soda
1/2 teaspoon baking powder
1/2 teaspoon salt
1/2 cup crushed pineapple, juice and all

Drop by teaspoon on greased cookie sheet. Bake at 350° about 10 minutes.

I've given your request for a recipe much thought. Practically every favorite recipe, and many just trial recipes, have already appeared in *The Eagle*. At present, our favorite recipes are those that are flavorful although low in cholesterol and fat.

At the moment, our two favorites are the Mock Veal Stew which appeared in *The Eagle* on May 6, 1991. I think that recipe came on a package of turkey cutlets. I use either chicken or turkey. Tom's all-time favorite since fried foods are restricted is what we call Corn Flake Chicken, skinned and boned chicken breasts, marinated in 7-up soda for about an hour, dipped in crushed corn flakes, sprinkled with a little melted margarine and baked at 350° for about 3/4 of an hour. Tom says this is as close to Southern Fried Chicken as we can come within his restrictions.

LEMON SQUARES
Frances Dichter

2 cups flour
½ c. butter or margarine
¼ c. confectioners sugar

Pre-heat oven to 350°. Mix first three ingredients well. Press into 8 inch square pan. Bake 20 - 25 minutes; do not overbake. Remove from oven. Cover with the following:

2 eggs
1 c. sugar
4 tbsp. lemon juice

1 tsp. baking powder
½ tbsp. confectioners sugar

Mix next four ingredients well. Beat until creamy. Spread evenly over baked layer in pan. Return to oven and bake 15 - 20 minutes.

Remove from oven and sift confectioners sugar over the top. Cool and cut into squares. May be frozen.

GINGER BREAD
Clifford Rudisill

This recipe is a variation of a coveted recipe of the Houston Club, Houston, Texas.

1 cup butter
1 cup sugar
2 cups molasses
8 eggs

4 cups flour
4 teaspoons baking powder
2 teaspoons baking soda
2 teaspoons cinnamon

8 teaspoons ginger
½ cup boiling water
1 cup raisins
2 teaspoons salt

Set oven at 350°. Grease/flour/Pam-Loaf Pans. Cream butter and sugar until fluffy. Beat in molasses and then add in eggs. Sift dry ingredients into batter. Blend well and add raisins, then boiling water until a smooth, creamy mix is achieved.

Bake 45 to 50 minutes until firm. Gently remove from pans when cooled for about 10 minutes. Use teflon pans if you have them. Makes 3 loaves.

MUSTER DAY GINGERBREAD
Marilyn Avery

These gingerbread cookies were an indispensable part of a New England tradition called "Muster Day." It was a day set aside for military training, but it became an occasion for festivity as well.

⅔ cup brown sugar, firmly packed	¾ tablespoon baking soda
⅔ cup molasses	⅔ cup butter
1 teaspoon ginger	1 egg
1 teaspoon cinnamon	5 cups all-purpose flour
½ teaspoon cloves	

Heat brown sugar, molasses, ginger, cinnamon, and cloves to the boiling point. Remove from heat, add baking soda (it foams) and pour over butter in a mixing bowl. Stir until butter has melted, then stir in the egg and flour thoroughly. Knead for a few minutes, then gather dough into a ball. Refrigerate until firm enough to roll easily (several hours or overnight). Roll on a lightly floured board to ¼ inch thickness and cut with large cookie cutters. Place on greased cookie sheet and bake in preheated 325° oven for 8 to 10 minutes. Do not overbake. Store in air-tight container so that they stay soft. At Christmas we decorate gingerbread people with piped pink frosting.

CHOCOLATE BREAD PUDDING
Barbara Morey

3 slices white bread in small pieces	1 cup milk
1 square bitter chocolate	pinch of salt
¼ cup sugar	1 egg well beaten
1 tbsp. butter	½ tsp. vanilla

Put bread, chocolate, sugar, butter, salt and milk in sauce pan over low heat. Cook until chocolate is melted. Add egg and vanilla. Mix and pour into greased baking dish. Bake 350°. for 25 - 30 minutes.

Serve with hard sauce made with 4 tbsp. butter and enough confectioner's sugar to make a sauce the consistency of whipped cream. Add 1 tsp. of vanilla.

BURNT SUGAR CAKE
Lee Stanfield

This recipe is in a cookbook published in 1933.

½ cup sugar
¼ cup hot water
3 cups cake flour
3 teaspoons baking powder
½ teaspoon salt
½ cup butter or other shortening

1½ cups sugar
3 egg yolks (well beaten)
1 cup water
1 teaspoon vanilla
2 tablespoons caramelized sugar syrup
3 egg whites, stiffly beaten

To make caramelized sugar syrup, place ½ cup sugar in skillet over medium heat and stir constantly until melted and quite dark. Remove from heat, add ¼ cup hot water, and stir until dissolved.

Sift flour, measure, add baking powder and salt; sift together three times (I always skipped this procedure).

LEMON CLOUD PIE
Ruth T. Degenhardt

Pillsbury Recipe circa 1968

One 9" Baked Pie Shell

Filling:
¾ cup sugar
¾ cup cornstarch
1 teaspoon grated lemon rind

1 cup water
⅓ cup lemon juice (2-3 lemons)
2 slightly beaten egg yolks

2 egg whites
¼ cup sugar
4 oz. cream cheese (cut into chunks for easier blending).

Cook: First six ingredients over medium heat stirring constantly, until thick. Remove from heat and stir in 4 oz. cream cheese. Blend well. Cool while preparing meringue.

Meringue: Beat 2 egg whites until they form soft peaks. *Gradually* beat in ¼ cup sugar, beating until stiff peaks form. Fold into lemon mixture using slotted spoon. Spoon into baked pie shell. Chill at least 2 hours.

CHRISTMAS PIE
Barbara Reddington

4 cups apples	pinch salt	2 crust pie
1 cup cranberries	½ teaspoon cinnamon	2 tablespoons flour
1 cup apricots	¼ teaspoon nutmeg	Butter on top
a cup sugar		

Bake at 425° for 5 minutes. 300° for 40 - 50 minutes (or until done)

CHOCOLATE MOUSSE PIE
Barbara Reddington

1 chocolate pie crust
1 12-oz. package Hershey's chocolate almond pie
1 pint whipped cream

Melt chocolate, whip cream, blend together. Pour into pie shell and chill.

STRAWBERRY PIE
Anne Everest Wojtkowski

Pie Crust
1¼ cups all-purpose flour
2 tablespoons sugar
¼ lb. margarine or butter
ice water

Filling
1½-2 qts. large strawberries
1 cup sugar
5 tablespoons cornstarch
water

Pie Crust Instructions: Mix flour and sugar in a medium bowl. With fingers, combine flour mixture with room temperature margarine until mixture is reduced to very small, coarse nodules whose content is consistent. Add egg yolk and about 2 tablespoons of very cold water. Work in with fingertips until dough just holds together. (The trick with all pie crusts is not to overwork once liquid has been added.) On a sheet of wax paper about 14" long, flatten dough until it is round and about 5" in diameter. Fold wax paper over dough and chill until firm. Unpack dough and top with another 14" sheet of wax paper. Roll between sheets of wax paper until it is about 12" in diameter. Remove top sheet. Turn crust over and into a 9" pie pan. Carefully remove wax paper. Press dough against all surfaces of pan. At rim, fold over excess and flute between thumb and forefinger so that crust extends above rim by about ½ inch. Chill for about ½ hour. Bake at 375° for fifteen minutes. After about 10 minutes, check crust and prick with fork whenever dough bubbles. Remove when lightly browned.

Filling: Place strawberries in a large bowl of cold water. Immediately hull and cut off any soft spots. Separate those well-formed and ripened berries to be used "as-is" for filling from those to be used, mashed-up, as "the glue." In the cooked and cooled pie crust, place one layer of the "as-is" strawberries, upside down, so that the stem sides are on the bottom. Arrange these strawberries as close together as possible. Where necessary, especially near rim, slice strawberries to fill in gaps.

To make "the glue": Mash up about one cup of loose strawberries; place in a 2-cup container; add water until mixture measures 1¾ cups. In a 3-quart pot, mix sugar and cornstarch. Add the mashed strawberries; place in a 2-cup container; add water until mixture measures 1¾ cups. In 1 three quart pot, mix sugar and cornstarch. Add the mashed strawberry mixture. Cook at medium-high heat, stirring constantly, until "glue" is thick and clear. Boil for one-to-two minutes. Remove from heat. Cool for about ½ hour, stirring occasionally. Pour "glue" over top of pie, making sure it completely surrounds the fresh berries. Chill for at least 2 hours. It is best served the same day it is made.

NOTE: This pie has been modified over the years from one my husband, Tom, and I ran into consistently in Nova Scotia on our honeymoon. It is well worth the effort. It is beautiful to look at and is a taste sensation.

CARROT CAKE
Anne Everest Wojtkowski

1½ cups grated, raw carrots, firmly packed (⅔ to ¾ pound)
1½ cups salad oil
2½ cups granulated sugar
4 egg yolks, unbeaten
5 tablespoons hot water
2½ cups sifted regular all purpose flour (2 cups rice flour if on a gluten-free diet)
1½ teaspoons double-acting baking powder
½ teaspoon baking soda
¼ teaspoon salt
1 teaspoon each: nutmeg, cinnamon, cloves
1 cup chopped pecans (about 4 ounces)
4 egg whites, beaten until soft peaks form

Glaze:
1 cup sifted confectioners' sugar
2 tablespoons lemon juice

Instructions: Preheat the oven to 350″. Grease and flour a 10 x 4½ inch cast aluminum Bundt cake pan. In a large bowl, with mixer at medium speed, cream salad oil and sugar until well mixed. Add egg yolks and beat well. Beat in hot water. Add grated carrots.

Sift flour with baking powder, baking soda, salt, nutmeg, cinnamon and cloves. Beat into carrot mixture at medium speed. Fold in by hand the beaten egg whites and pecans. Pour into pan. Bake 50 to 55 minutes. Do not overcook. Cool in pan 15 minutes, then remove and turn over onto a cake plate and let cool another 10-20 minutes.

Drizzle frosting on top, letting frosting run down the sides. Note on the frosting: The idea is to achieve a consistency that will just barely flow when spread on the warm cake, but harden before it has run off the cake. If frosting appears to be liquid, add more confectioner's sugar.

ZUCCHINI CHOCOLATE CAKE
Marilyn Avery

½ cup butter or margarine softened
½ cup vegetable oil
1¾ cup sugar
2 whole eggs
1 teaspoon vanilla
½ cup sour milk (add 1 tsp. lemon juice to regular milk)
2½ cup flour

4 tablespoons cocoa
½ teaspoon baking powder
1 teaspoon baking soda
1 tablespoon cinnamon
½ teaspoon cloves or allspice
2 cups shredded zucchini
1 6 oz. bag chocolate chips

Cream margarine, oil and sugar. Add eggs, vanilla and sour milk and beat with the mixer until well blended. In another bowl, mix together all dry ingredients and add to creamed mixture. Stir in zucchini.

Spoon into greased 9 x 13 pan and sprinkle top with chocolate chips. Bake at 325 degrees for 40 - 50 minutes until toothpick inserted neat center of cake comes out clean. Squirt of whipped cream compliments taste of spicy chocolate.

BERTHA EDDY'S POUND CAKE

8 large eggs
1¾ cups sweet butter
2⅓ cups granulated sugar
3¼ cups white flour
½ tsp. mace
2 tbsp. brandy

Cream butter and sugar until light and fluffy. Separate eggs and beat egg whites until stiff. Add yolks one at a time to creamed butter and sugar and beat thoroughly after each addition. Stir in mace and brandy. Add flour, measured after sifting, and mix well. Stir in ⅓ of beaten egg whites and carefully fold in balance. No egg whites should show in smooth batter. Pour batter into buttered and floured loaf pan(s) and bake in moderate oven for 80 minutes. Test with toothpick or cake tester to be sure cake is done. Allow to cool in pan for five minutes and turn out on rack to cool completely. Store in air tight container where it will remain fresh for a week or longer.

N.B. This old recipe was modified by Bertha Eddy before 1900 from one which listed as ingredients: 10 eggs, 1 pound butter, 1 pound sugar, 1 pound flour, ½ teaspoon mace and 2 tablespoons brandy. No directions were given except: "Bake in moderate oven for 80 minutes." Further modifications could include adding 1 tsp. baking powder to sifted flour, adding 1 tsp. vanilla extract with mace and brandy, omitting the brandy, or adding ½ tsp. salt with flour. (Ground mace is considered essential for an authentic pound cake.) The egg yolks may be beaten until thickened and light yellow (after whites have been beaten) and added to creamed butter and sugar all together. The batter may also be baked as a sheet cake from which to make petits fours in which case it will take only 30 minutes.

TABLE OF CONTENTS   ADDENDA
SAUCES RELISHES CONDIMENTS   OLD SOURCES

She found a little restaurant smelling of olive-oil and garlic where diners still lingered, and a saffron mound of rice and fish was set before Vance. He revelled in the high seasoned diet, the thick sunny wine.

EDITH WHARTON, *THE GODS ARRIVE*

The greatest pleasure may be taken, by the philosopher and naturalist (and the farmer should be both) in contemplating that benign process by which ingredients the most offensive to the human senses are converted into articles that gratify the most delicate taste, and pamper the most luxurious appetite.

HERMAN MELVILLE,
REPORT OF THE COMMITTEE ON AGRICULTURE (1850)

APPLE GINGER
(with preserved ginger)
Frances Melville Thomas, daughter of Herman Melville.

4 lbs. apples
¾ cup finely chopped preserved ginger
¼ cup preserved ginger syrup
3 lemons
Granulated sugar

Pare, core and chop apples fine. Combine with the ginger, the ginger syrup and the lemon chopped after the seeds have been removed. Weigh this mixture and combine with an equal weight of sugar (or add 3 lbs. sugar) in a large kettle. To make the preserve richer and more seasoned, let it stand overnight. In the morning let it simmer for three hours or until the pieces of fruit are soft. Pour into hot jelly glasses and seal. Fills six 8 ounce jelly glasses.
Frances Melville Thomas's cook prepared this for the daughter of Herman Melville. Presented by Melville Chapin, the grandson of Herman Melville, from copies of family recipes.

There is another class of foods, called condiments, which should not pass unnoticed.[6]

Food that "tastes good" is digested more readily, and assimilated more perfectly, so that we really derive more nourishment from it. We use many articles with our food to make it taste better, which are not in themselves valuable food. But by stimulating the flow of saliva and gastric juice, and enhancing the fine flavor of food, they increase the pleasure of eating, and render digestion more complete. These are called condiments. They are not necessary to persons of sound digestion, and with the exception of salt, should not be used by children, nor by any one in large quantities. In perfect digestion, there is the first taste in the mouth and the after-taste of the digestive organs which require satisfaction. "Any cook may gratify the first, but the second requires a skilled chemist."[16]

TOMATO CATSUP

7 pounds tomatoes - ripe
4 tablespoons salt
4 tablespoons black pepper
3 tablespoons mustard

½ tablespoon allspice
½ tablespoons on cloves
1 pint vinegar

Boil three or four hours.[5]

RIPE TOMATOES (Pickles)

7 pounds tomatoes
3 pounds sugar
2 quarts vinegar
cloves and cinnamon

Scald the vinegar 3 mornings in succession.[5]

PICKLED CHOW CHOW

1 gallon green tomatoes chopped fine
4 green peppers
4 onions
A handful of salt sprinkled on them.

Let stand for six hours then drain off the juice. Add 1 tablespoon of ground pepper, also one of allspice, 1 of cloves, 3 of mace, ½ pint of mustard seed and 3 pints of vinegar.[5]

MINCE PIES
Mrs. A. Hamms, Worcester

Two and a half pounds of beef
One and a half pounds suet
2 pounds sugar
2 pounds raisins
8 large apples
brandy
spices[5]

GREEN TOMATO MINCEMEAT FOR PIES

Chop fine one peck tomatoes, drain off juice, add as much cold water as there was juice, scald up, drain off water, scald again and pour off the water. Add 4 lbs of brown sugar, 2 lbs. chopped raisins, 2 cups of chopped beef suet, 2 tablespoons salt. Cook until done. Add 1 cup of vinegar. When partly cold, add 2 level tablespoons cinnamon, 2 level tablespoons clove, 1 level tablespoon nutmeg. This makes seven quarts of mincemeat.[12]

MINCE MEAT
Mrs. M.C. Richmond

Two pounds of tongue, two pounds of fresh lean beef, weighing them after they are chopped, four pounds of chopped tart apples, weighing them after they are pared and cored; four pounds or raisins stoned and chopped, not too fine; two pounds of currants, picked over, well washed and then rubbed dry in a clean towel and sifted to free them from stems; one pound of citron cut in small thin slices, quarter of a pound each of candied orange and lemon peel, sliced thin, one pound of sweet almonds and two ounces of bitter almonds, weighed after the shells are removed, blanch the almonds by pouring boiling water over them after they are shelled, and then rubbing the skin off with a clean towel, chop them, not too fine, add four pounds of sugar, season with two level tablespoonfuls of salt, one level teaspoonful each of pepper, ground cloves, allspice, cinnamon and mace, and two medium-size nutmegs grated, next add three-fourths of a quart each of currant and raspberry jelly, and the juice the meat was boiled in, mix thoroughly, and let it stand at least one day before using it. If covered and placed where it is cool, this will keep all winter.[2]

TOMATO DINNER SAUCE

Seven pounds of ripe tomatoes, two and a half pounds sugar, one pint of vinegar, one-half ounce of different spices. Put in a bag, boil slowly three hours or more, grate a nutmeg. A little onion if you like.[9]

CHILI SAUCE

Ten ripe tomatoes chopped fine, three green peppers, two onions chopped fine, one cup of vinegar, one-half cup sugar, one tablespoonful of salt, one teaspoon of pepper, one of mace, one of cloves, one of all-spice, one of nutmeg. Bottle for use.[9]

Chapped Hands. - One ounce alcohol, one ounce glycerine, one ounce cologne, one ounce tarsgacanth. Dissolve the last in a little water, then add hot water: when dissolved and hot add other ingredients.[8]

For the King's Evil. Take as much cream of tartar as will lie on a Sixpence, every morning and Evening.[1]

GRAPE CATSUP

Grapes boiled and collandered, five pounds; sugar, two and a half pounds; vinegar, one pint; cinnamon, cloves, allspice and pepper, one tablespoon of each; one-half tablespoon of salt. Boil until sufficiently thick.[9]

CHOW-CHOW

To one peck of green tomatoes finely chopped add one teacupful of salt over night. The next day drain the water off, add three onions and three peppers, also chopped, three tablespoonfuls of ground cloves, three of cinnamon, one of ground mustard, six of white mustard seed, and one and a half cups of grated horse radish. Cover it with vinegar and keep from the air.[9]

PICCADILLY

One peck of sliced green tomatoes, cover with water and a pinch of salt, let them stand twelve hours, turn that off and rinse with fresh water, remove parts of the seeds, twelve green peppers, one large head of cabbage chopped fine and mix well, add weak vinegar and scald, then drain your vinegar off and add grated horse radish, one pint mustard seed, one tablespoon of ground cloves, one of allspice, one of sugar, put in a jar, cover with cold water.[9]

NASTURTIUM PICKLE

Pick the nasturtium seeds green; leave a short stem on them and place them in a weak brine for two days; then soak them in fresh water for a day. Pack them in jars and turn over them in boiling vinegar; seal and let them stand a month before using.[16]

RICH PUDDING SAUCE
(For Fruit Puddings or Croquettes.)

3 tablespoonfuls of butter
3 tablespoonfuls of powdered sugar
2 tablespoonfuls of hot water
½ cup of sherry

juice of ½ lemon
2 egg yolks
dash of nutmeg

Cream the butter; add the sugar, and cream again thoroughly; then add the yolks and beat until light; add the hot water and the nutmeg. Place it in a saucepan of hot water, and beat, adding slowly the lemon-juice and the wine. The sauce should be foamy.[16]

FOAMY SAUCE
(Steamed and baked pudding.)

½ cupful of butter
1 cupful of powdered sugar
1 teaspoonful of vanilla

¼ cupful of boiling water
2 tablespoonfuls of sherry
1 egg white

Cream the butter and sugar; add the vanilla and wine, and beat them well. Just before serving stir in the boiling water; add the whipped white of one egg, and beat until foamy.[16]

PICKLES AND PRESERVES

"Bring forth, therefore, fruits meet for repentance."[9]

For pickles, the BEST CIDER VINEGAR is necessary, and it should be used COLD. Spices may be used if liked.[9]

PICKLED RAISINS

A layer of raisins, a little sugar and spice, and scalding vinegar to cover them.[9]

FRENCH PICKLE

Slice a peck of green tomatoes and six large onions. Let them stand over night in salt. Drain them well and cook in a quart of vinegar and two quarts of water for fifteen or twenty minutes. Drain again. Add two quarts of vinegar, two pounds of brown sugar, one-half pound mustard seed, one tablespoon of cloves, one of ground mustard, one of cinnamon, one of allspice, one of ginger, one teaspoon red pepper. Boil fifteen minutes.[9]

SWEET PICKLED TOMATOES

One pint vinegar and one pound of sugar to four pounds of fruit. Scald tomatoes in salt and water, then drain and place in the jar. Then put sugar and vinegar in a kettle on the stove, then spices as follows: Cinnamon, cloves and white mustard seed, and one red pepper. Let them scald thoroughly and pour on the tomatoes, keeping them covered.[9]

SLIP

One tablespoonful cornstarch, one pint boiling water, one small cup sugar, juice and rind of one lemon; boil all together until thick, and pour in baking dish; beat the white of the egg with tablespoonful of sugar, spread on top; brown slightly and serve cold, with cold boiled custard.[8]

TARTAR SAUCE
Mrs. M.J. Rice

Add to ½ cup good salad dressing, ½ teaspoon minced onion. 1 tablespoon chopped parsley, 1 tablespoon finely chopped sour pickle. 1 tablespoon finely chopped olives. Beat this mixture well, and keep on ice till ready to serve.[12]

CHEESE SAUCE
Mrs. M.S. Haviland

To serve with rice croquettes or egg omelette. Melt 2 tablespoons butter in saucepan, stir in 2 tablespoon flour and slowly add 1½ cups milk, stirring constantly. Bring to boiling point, season with salt and paprika. Add ½ cup finely chopped cheese, stir till cheese is melted. More cheese may be used, but not over 1 cup.[12]

A most delicious sauce, called "Shoyu," which is in the basis of Worcestershire sauce, is also used to give spice to the food. Throughout the repast the guests are served from time to time with "Saki," a pale liquor made from rice, and which tastes very much like sherry. It is served hot, and is a most insinuating tipple. In a large party you are expected to exchange cups and drink with every one present. The result is that, in nine cases out of ten, you leave the house just a "wee bit fu'," as they say in Scotland. Like the Chinese, no knives, forks, or napkins are used -- "chop sticks" only. To smack your lips or belch during the feast is, strange to say of such a supremely polite people, not considered bad form. [4]

CARAMEL
Mrs. M.S. Haviland

To color gravies and soups. 1 cup sugar moistened with water, then burned in saucepan over fire (cold water will clean the saucepan); add one pint boiling water. Cool and bottle. Will keep indefinitely.[12]

AMBER MARMALADE
Miss Siebells

1 large grapefruit
2 large oranges
1 lemon

1st day: Wash and dry the fruits. With a very sharp knife, cut the fruit into halves, then quarters, then in very thin slices. Using a cooking vessel in which the fruit is to be cooked. Measure the fruit, and to each cup of fruit, add 1 cup cold water. Cover, let stand all night.

2nd day: Cook until the fruit is tender. Cool. Cover, and let stand until the next day.

3rd day: Measure the fruit. To each cup of fruit (juice, pulp, rind) add ¾ of a cup of sugar. (Unless you like it very sweet, if so use 1 cup of sugar). Let cook briskly until it boils, lower the flame, and let simmer from two to 2½ hours. Stir frequently, skim whenever necessary. Cook until the consistency of jam. Pour into glasses. Set aside to cool and the following morning, pour melted parafine wax over the top.[12]

CARROT CONSERVE
Martha Waterman

1½ quarts of cooked diced carrots, rind of 2 lemons, juice of 3 lemons, 5 cups of sugar, 2 cups of hot water. Boil carrots until tender then put through chopper, with lemon rind, mix with sugar water and lemon juice, and boil until thick.[12]

STRAWBERRY CONSERVE
Mrs. Hannah A. Bailey

5 qts. berries
5 lbs. of sugar
2 pineapples
2 oranges
¼ lb. English walnuts

Boil slowly ½ hour.[12]

FIG AND PEAR CONSERVE
N.H. Ashley

5 lbs. pears
3 lbs. sugar
1 lb. figs

Pare and slice pears, add chopped figs and sugar and a little water. Cook slowly until thick.[12]

Seats of cane chairs that have become baggy will tighten again if they are washed in very hot soda water and put outside to dry in the sun and wind.[3]

Skimmed Milk is a good starch for calicoes.[3]

Lemon juice and vinegar, used in moderation, increase the solvent properties of the gastric juices, and are useful with meats and vegetables which are difficult of digestion.[6]

GREEN TOMATO CONSERVE
Mrs. Ceila M. Sears

2 qts. of sliced green tomatoes
3 lemons, remove the white skin of each
3 lbs. of sugar
a little ginger root
1 orange
1 lb. of raisins
English walnuts

Cook slowly until thick.[12]

GRAPE CONSERVE
Mrs. Jules Dupont

1 basket of Concord grapes
2 oranges (all but seeds, put through medium chopper)
3 lbs. sugar
1 package of raisins
¼ lb. or 1 cup English walnuts shelled (put through coarse chopper)

Slip skins from grapes and cool pulp about 5 minutes, strain, then put pulp, skins, raisins, oranges and sugar on to cook and cook until like jelly. Add nuts 5 minutes before turning into glasses.[12]

ADDENDA SAUCES RELISHES CONDIMENTS CONTEMPORARY SOURCES

CRISP WATERMELON PICKLES

4 quarts peeled, trimmed-of-all-red-flesh and cut-up-into-small-squares watermelon rind (that's the rind from 1 large watermelon)
1 teaspoon alum
1.2 teaspoon salt
Water (see below for amount)
1 quart cider vinegar
4 pounds sugar
4 cinnamon sticks, broken
16 whole cloves
2 thinly sliced lemons

Put the prepared watermelon rind, the alum and the salt in a very large pot. Add enough water to cover. Boil until the rind is tender, about ½ hour. Drain thoroughly, then cool in ice-cold water. Drain again. When dry, divide the rind between 4 1-pint canning jars.[19]

THE BOUNTIFUL PANTRY
Glenn Andrew - Food from Heartland

Now put the cider vinegar and sugar in a large pot along with 2 cups of water. Bring to a boil, then add the cinnamon sticks, cloves, and lemon slices, all tied in a cheesecloth bag. Boil together until the syrup becomes clear, then remove the spice bag and divide the boiling syrup between the jars. (Most people discard the spices at this point, but I like the look of a piece of cinnamon stick and a couple of cloves in each jar, so I open the spice bag and add them.)

Seal the jars at once (see page 194) and try to refrain from using the pickles for about a month, when they'll fully flavored. Makes about 4 1-pint jars.

DILLED GREEN BEANS
Richard Dunn-Pittsfield Unitarian Universalist 1989 Cookbook

3 lb. whole green beans
1½ tsp. cayenne pepper
6 garlic cloves
6 dill heads or 2 tbl. dill seed

3½ cups vinegar
3½ cups water
3 tablespoons salt

Add 1 clove garlic, 1 head dill and ¼ teaspoon cayenne to bottom of each clean hot pint jar. Wash beans and cut off ends. Pack lengthwise in jars, leaving ¼ inch of headroom. In enameled kettle mix water, vinegar and salt. Bring to boil and pour boiling hot over beans in jars. Leave ¼ inch of headroom. Adjust lids and process in boiling water bath (212°) for ten minutes.

It takes about 2 weeks for full flavor to develop. The added vinegar raises the naturally low-acid beans to the strong-acid category, so a boiling water bath is adequate for safe processing.

ANNE'S EGGPLANT RELISH
(No fat, no salt, no sugar)
Anne Everest Wojtkowski

Eggplant steamed, peeled, cut into one-inch cubes
1 large onion
2 large cloves garlic, crushed
1 large can tomato
1 green pepper
Generous basil and oregano

Steam. Reserve until next day. Improves with time.

CONFETTI CORN RELISH
Glenn Andrews - Food from Heartland ©

It's hard to find any corn relish at all in stores, let alone one as beautiful both to look at and taste as this one. Some people add shredded cabbage to their corn relish, but this seems to me to muddy the looks and the flavor. I prefer this version of an old Wisconsin recipe, which is similar to the corn relishes we took along to go with the ham, that was served on most of our picnics in Iowa. The prepared mustard it contains is its real secret.

12 ears corn, cooked
4 large stalks celery, finely chopped
2 large onions, finely chopped
1 large green pepper, finely chopped
1 large sweet red pepper, finely chopped
1½ cups light or dark brown sugar
1½ cups cider or white vinegar
½ cup prepared (bought, that is) yellow mustard
1 teaspoon dry mustard
1 tablespoon flour
2 tablespoons salt

Cut the kernels from the ears of corn and put into a large pot with all the other ingredients. (Save the corncobs to make Corncob Jelly or Corncob Syrup.) Bring to a boil, stirring, then turn the heat down and simmer for about 30 minutes, stirring every five minutes. Pour into freshly sterilized jars and process in a hot water bath. Makes about 4 pints.[19]

PICO de GALLO (Homemade Salsa)
Janet Cook

Salsa freshly made with in-season tomatoes beats the commercial brands every time. Cilantro gives it a unique and authentic taste, but if you can't find it, substitute fresh parsley. Make a large quantity and save.

1 large tomato, chopped fine
1 small onion, chopped fine
1-2 tablespoons chopped canned jalapenos (or to taste)
2 tablespoons fresh cilantro, chopped

Chop and combine all ingredients. Place in small serving bowl. Per full recipe: Calories: 80 Fat (grams): trace Saturated Fat: 0 Cholesterol (mgs.): 0 Variations/Suggestions: Serve with toasted corn tortilla wedges (instead of high-fat corn chips).

EGGPLANT CAPONATA
Maureen Stapleton

1 medium eggplant
salt
2 onions chopped
¾ cup olive oil
2 cloves garlic, finely chopped
1 one-pound can Italian plum tomatoes, strained
2 stalks celery, coarsely chopped
8 large pitted green olives, quartered
¼ cup capers
2 tablespoons pignoli (pine nuts)
2 tablespoons wine vinegar
Additional salt and freshly ground black pepper to taste.

1. Wash the eggplant and leaving the skin on, cut it into one-inch cubes. Sprinkle the eggplant cubes with salt and let stand one hour. Rinse and dry.

2. Put cubes in heated oil and cook the eggplant over low heat until soft. Remove the eggplant from the oil and set aside.

3. Add the onions, garlic, tomatoes, celery, and green olives to the pan with the oil. Cook until the celery is crisp tender.

4. Add the eggplant, capers, pine nuts, and vinegar to the celery-olive mixture. Season to taste with salt and pepper. Chill thoroughly before serving.

CHOCOLATE SAUCE FOR ICE CREAM OR CAKE
Jane P. Fitzpatrick

1 square unsweetened baking chocolate
2 tablespoons butter or margarine (size of a walnut!)
⅓ cup boiling water
1 cup sugar
1 dash salt
1 teaspoon vanilla

Melt chocolate and butter slowly. Add boiling water and stir until slightly thickened. Add sugar and bring to a boil over medium heat. Add salt and vanilla. Now it's ready to serve on ice cream or cake; REALLY NEEDS TO BE WARM TO BE DELICIOUS.

MORNAY SAUCE
Janet Cook

Heat in copper bottom pan so milk will not stick:
1 quart milk
1 bay leaf (discard when milk is hot)

Melt in a small pan: 6 tablespoons butter. Blend well into butter to make a roux: 9½ tablespoons flour (be exact with this), 2½ teaspoons herb salt, good dash white pepper. Add roux to heated milk, stirring constantly with wire whip until it thickens, then add and cook one minute: 1 egg yolk, mixed well in ¼ cup coffee cream. When done, add and stir in, mixing thoroughly: 2½ tablespoons sherry, 3 ounces sharp cheddar, grated fine, ¼ teaspoon Worcestershire sauce, dash cayenne pepper. Then reheat, stirring constantly to blend all ingredients. This sauce is so good for so many uses that a large amount can be made and kept in the refrigerator for at least a week without spoiling. All that is necessary when you want to use some is to put it in a double boiler and reheat it.

FRESH MUSHROOM SAUCE
Maureen Stapleton

Cook until mushy: 2 tablespoons butter, 1 clove garlic, minced, ½ cup onions, sliced. When onions start to get brown in color, add and cook until well done: ½ pound fresh mushrooms, sliced; 1 tablespoon flour, mixed in ½ cup water, ½ teaspoon lemon or lime juice. For a variation of this recipe, instead of adding the flour and citrus juice, use ½ cup of commercial sour cream and stir in well. The mushrooms should be cooked down to a good consistency for this, or the addition of the sour cream will make the mixture too thin. Served over omelettes or added to cooked rice, this recipe serves 4.

APPLE BUTTER
Glenn Andrews - Food from the Heartland ©

Making this spread was a family event since many hands were needed to stir the butter constantly for hours to prevent it from scorching. As the butter thickened, it began to spit and to get all over everything within reach. For this reason, Apple Butter making was usually done outdoors. Today, though, the butter is generally made in the oven, a major laborsaving move.

4 pounds apples, peeled, cored and sliced
1 cup water
1 cup sharp apple cider or cider vinegar
1 cup sugar or honey
1 teaspoon cinnamon
1 teaspoon ground cloves
1 teaspoon ground allspice

Cook the apples in the water and cider or cider vinegar until very soft, then add the rest of the ingredients and put in a large fairly shallow pan in a 350° F oven. Bake, stirring every 20 minutes, for about 3 hours, or until thick.

Pack in freshly sterilized jars and process in a hot water bath. Makes about 6 8-ounce jars. (By fruit butter standards, this is a small batch, but this recipe can be doubled or tripled.) [19]

DILL SAUCE
Jytte Brooks

3 tablespoons (50 g) Dijon mustard
1 cup (240 ml) olive oil
2 tablespoons (30 g) sugar
½ cup (20 g) or 4 sprigs fresh dill
1 teaspoon (5 ml) vinegar

Chop dill in food processor and add mustard, sugar and vinegar. While machine is running, pour oil in little by little through the tube. This makes a thick sauce which is very good served with any kind of cold fish dish.

EPILOGUE PUDDINGS DESSERTS CONFECTIONS OLD SOURCES

They frequented, where attended by the troubled Gerty, she lunched luxuriously, as she said, on her expectations.
"My dear Gerty, you wouldn't have me let the headwaiter see that I've nothing to live on but Aunt Julia's legacy? Think of Grace Stepney's satisfaction if she came in and found us lunching on cold mutton and tea! What sweet shall we have today, dear—Coup Jacques or Peaches a la Melba?"

EDITH WHARTON, *HOUSE OF MIRTH*

From the recipe book of Mrs. William Cullen Bryant dated 1831

INDIAN PUDDING - Baked

Scald two quarts of milk. Stir in 1 pint of Indian meal, or enough to make a good mush, and a little salt. A teacup of molasses, a tablespoon of ginger. A little of any other spices if you like.

AMHERST PUDDING

One cup of butter and lard, one cup molasses, one cup sweet milk, one cup seedless raisins, three cups flour, one-half teaspoonful of soda, one teaspoonful cinnamon, one teaspoonful salt. Boil in a tight pail placed in a larger one for three hours continuously. This is good steamed over.

Sauce: Two teaspoonfuls butter, one teaspoonful of flour, one pinch of salt. Rub well together over the stove until it creams, than turn in one and one-half cups of boiling water and let it boil a few minutes, stirring all the time; then stir in the yolk of one egg and one cup of sugar rubbed until creamy; let it cool, then add the beaten white of the egg. Flavor with vanilla.[8]

SURPRISE PUDDING

Cut four thin slices of bread from a five-cent loaf, or its equivalent from a home-made loaf. Butter the bread and lay in a buttered earthen pudding dish. Beat together, one egg, one-third cup sugar, four tablespoonfuls molasses and three cups of milk; pour over the bread. Let stand half hour or more, than bake in slow oven (1½) one and one-half hours; cover at first. Serve with liquid sauce or cream.[8]

From a book of handwritten recipes which was found in the Hyde family homestead on West Park Street in Lee. The house was built in 1792 by the Reverend Alvan Hyde, pastor of the Congregational Church in Lee and Vice President of Williams College. Upon Reverend Hyde's death, his youngest son, Alexander, inherited the house in which he conducted a "family boarding school" which included among its students the father of President Franklin D. Roosevelt. Alexander's daughter, Adeline Hyde Marsh, moved into the house in the 1880s and lived there until her death in 1933. She and her daughter, Harriet, collected the recipes from which several have been selected for inclusion in this book. Members of the Hyde Family continued to live in the house until 1933.

COFFEE CREAM

1 quart of milk   3 eggs
1 pint strong coffee   1 cup sugar
½ box gelatin

Mix the milk and the coffee together and let boil for ten or fifteen minutes. Then beat the yolks very light putting them with the boiling mixture, with the gelatin and sugar. Let it cook until the gelatin is dissolved; then take off the stove to cool. Beat the whites until lightened, strain the mixture onto them cutting the whites in. Then pour into molds to cool. This is very nice served with whipped cream.

IRISH MOSS BLANC MANGE

Take a small handful of Irish moss, soak it in water bloodwarm for 2 hours. Take moss out and put it in a quart of milk. Boil ten or fifteen minutes until the moss is nearly melted. Sweeten and add a little rose water. Strain in the mold to cool. Some boil a stick of cinnamon with the milk.[5]

"Man wants but little here below."

Plain food is quite enough for me;
Three courses are as good as ten—
If Nature can subsist on three,
Thank Heaven for three. Amen!
I always thought cold victual nice—
My CHOICE would be vanilla-ice.

OLIVER WENDELL HOLMES
CONTENTMENT

Nor was that most wonderful object of domestic art called "trifle" wanting, with the charming confusion of cream and cake and almonds and jam and jelly and wine and cinnamon and froth; nor yet the marvelous "floating island", name suggestions of all that is romantic in the imagination of youthful palates.

OLIVER WENDELL HOLMES,
ELSIE VENNER

BREAD PUDDING

Take layers of bread and butter, then a layer of raisins, sugar, nutmeg, and cinnamon. Pour milk over to soak. Add eggs.

Sauce: ½ cup butter, 1 cup white sugar. Stir to a cream. Heat—just before serving. Boiling water, grate nutmeg on top.[5]

CRACKER PUDDING

2 quarts milk
9 crackers
4 eggs
2 teaspoons full cinnamon
1 teaspoon nutmeg
¼ cup molasses
1½ cups sugar
butter the size of an egg
pinch of soda

Stir when half done. Bake slowly for 6 hours.[5]

CHRISTMAS PLUM PUDDING

Mrs. J.M. Towne

One pint and a half of grated bread crumbs (soft, not dried).
One pint of chopped suet
One pint and a half of currants and stoned raisins mixed
½ cup of citron shaved thin
One scant cup of sugar
½ teaspoon of salt
½ teaspoon of grated nutmeg
5 eggs
2 even tablespoons of flour

Make into a thin batter with milk, and half a glass of brandy. Mix in the order given, and boil or steam four hours. Serve with yellow sauce.[16]

TURKISH DELIGHT
Ruth Reynolds

Soak 1 package Knox gelatin in 1 cup cold water. Pour 1½ cups boiling water on 2 lbs. sugar. Combine the two mixtures and boil 15 minutes. Boil like jelly and watch carefully. Wet a pan under cold water and pour mixture into it. Then add coloring and flavor (wintergreen, cinnamon, clove, etc.) Let stand over night. In the morning place on stove a second to loosen and cut with a silver knife dipped in hot water. Roll in either confectioner's or granulated sugar. [12]

HASTY PUDDING

Put on water according to the size of your family. Sift five or six spoonfuls of meal into a bowl of water, and when the kettle boils, stir it in and let it boil up thick. Then stand over the kettle and sprinkle in meal, handful after handful, stirring it thoroughly all the time. When it is so thick the pudding stick stands up in it, it is about right. Cook half an hour. Eat it with milk or molasses. Either Indian meal or rye meal may be used. Rye hasty pudding and West Indian molasses as a diet, would save many a one the horrors of dyspepsia.[1]

SWEET CORN PUDDING
Miss Eliza Williams

Take twelve ears of corn, cut the rows through the center and scrape out the pulp. Add three eggs, a pint of milk, and a spoonful of butter. Sweeten and flavor, and bake half an hour.[1]

TO MAKE FONDANT

Place in a copper or graniteware saucepan two cupfuls of granulated sugar, one cupful of water, and a scant half saltspoonful of cream of tartar. Stir until the sugar is dissolved, but not a minute longer. As it boils, a thin scum of crystals will form around the edge of the pan. These must be wiped away by wetting a cloth or brush in water, and passing it around the dish without touching the boiling sugar. This must be done frequently, or as often as the crystals form, or the whole mass will become granular. When large bubbles rise it must be carefully watched and tested, as from this time it quickly passes from one stage to another. Have a cup of ice-water and a skewer or small stick; dip it into the water, then into the sugar, and again into the water. If the sugar which adheres to it can be rolled into a soft ball, it is done. This is the stage of small-ball, and the thermometer registers 236°–238°. Have ready a marble slab, very lightly but evenly rubbed over with sweet-oil. If a slab is not at hand, a large platter will serve the purpose. The moment the sugar is done, pour it over the slab and let it cool a few minutes, or until, pressing it with the finger, it leaves a dent on the surface. If stirred while too warm it will grain. If a crust forms, every particle of it must be taken off, or else the boiling must be done again, as it shows it has cooked a little too long. When it will dent, work it with a wooden spatula, keeping the mass in the center as much as possible. Continue to stir until it becomes a very fine smooth, fine, white creamy paste, which is soft and not brittle and can be worked in the hands like a thick paste. If the results are not right and the mass becomes grained, the sugar need not be wasted, but can be put in the saucepan with a spoonful of water and boiled again. In stirring the fondant do mix in the scrapings unless the whole is still very soft. They can be worked by themselves afterward. Confectioners use one part of glucose to ten of sugar and boil at 240°.[16]

BAKED OR BOILED ARROWROOT PUDDING

Ingredients:
2 tablespoonfuls of arrowroot
1½ pint of milk
1 oz. of butter
½ lemon rind
2 heaped tablespoons moist sugar
a little grated nutmeg

Mode. - Mix the arrowroot with as much cold milk as will make it into a smooth batter, moderately thick; put the remainder of the milk into a stewpan with the lemon-peel, and let it infuse for about ½ hour; when it boils, strain it gently to the batter, stirring it all the time to keep it smooth; then add the butter; beat this well in until thoroughly mixed, and sweeten with moist sugar. Put the mixture into a pie dish, round which has been placed a border of paste (a rich dough), grate a little nutmeg over the top and bake the top, and bake the pudding from 1 to ¼ hour, in a moderate oven, or boil it the same length of time in a well-buttered basin. To enrich this pudding, stir to the other ingredients, just before it is put in the oven, 3 well-whisked eggs, and add a tablespoonful of brandy. For a nursery pudding, the addition of the latter ingredients will be found quite superfluous, as also the paste round the ends of the dish.

Time. - 1 to 1¼ hour, baked or boiled. Average cost, 7d. Sufficient for 5 or 6 persons. Seasonable at any time.[18]

ARROWROOT. - In India, and in the colonies, by the process of rasping, they extract from a vegetable (Maranta arundinacea) a sediment nearly resembling tapioca. The grated pulp is sifted into a quantity of water, from which it is afterwards strained and dried, and the sediment this produced is called Arrowroot. Its qualities closely resemble those of tapioca.[18]

BAKED APRICOT PUDDING

Ingredients. - 12 large apricots, ¾ pint of bread crumbs, 1 pint of milk, 3 oz. of pounded sugar, the yolks of 4 eggs, 1 glass of sherry.

Mode. - Make the milk boiling hot, and pour it on to the bread crumbs; when half cold, add the sugar, the well-whisked yolks of the eggs, and the sherry. Divide the apricots in half, scald them until they are soft, and break them up with a spoon, adding a few of the kernels, which should be well pounded in a mortar; then mix the fruit and other ingredients together, put a border of paste round the dish; fill with the mixture, and bake the pudding from ½ to ¾ hour.

Average cost, in full season, 1s. 6 d. Sufficient for 4 or 5 persons. Seasonable in August, September, and October.[18]

SEA FOAM
Madeline G. Booth

2 cups brown sugar
½ cup water
1 egg white
1 teaspoon vanilla
½ cup chopped nuts

Boil sugar and water together, till a little dropped in cold water forms a soft ball. Pour the hot mixture over the stiffly beaten white of an egg, beating while pouring. Add nuts and extract and beat till the candy stiffens. When nearly set, drop by spoonsful on paper.[12]

A BACHELOR'S PUDDING

Ingredients. - 4 oz. of grated bread, 4 oz. of currants, 4 oz. of apples, 2 oz. of sugar, 3 eggs, a few drops of essence of lemon, a little grated nutmeg.

Mode. - Pare, core, and mince the apples very finely, sufficient, when minced, to make 4 oz.; add to these the currants, which should be well washed, the grated bread, and sugar; which the eggs, beat these up with the remaining ingredients, and when all is thoroughly mixed, put the pudding into a buttered basin, tie it down with a cloth, and boil for 3 hours.

Time. - 3 hours. Average cost, 9d. Sufficient for 4 or 5 persons. Seasonable from August to March. [18]

TAPIOCA PUDDING

Arrange evenly in a buttered dish six apples which have been pared and cored. Any other fruit may be used—canned peaches are good. Soak a cupful of tapioca in hot water for an hour or more; sweeten and flavor it to taste and pour it over the fruit. Bake in a moderate oven for an hour. [16]

PLAIN RICE PUDDING NO. 1

In a pudding-dish holding a quart, put two heaping tablespoonfuls of well-washed rice; fill the dish with milk, and add a half teaspoonful of salt. Let it cook in the oven for half an hour, stirring it two or three times. Take it out and add two tablespoonfuls of sugar and a scant teaspoonful of vanilla; also a half cupful of stoned raisins if desired. Grate nutmeg over the top; return the dish to the oven and cook slowly for two hours or more; as the milk boils down, lift the skin at the side and add more hot milk. The pudding should be creamy, and this is attained by slow cooking, and using plenty of milk. [16]

A clever woman with an eye to Economy conceived the idea of "Ready Made Pies," obtained without heating the oven. On general baking days she baked one or two shells of paste which were set away in a dry, cool place. When fresh pies were wanted she simply mixed the custard which was lemon, chocolate or even pumpkin, cooked it over the top burner and then allowed it to become perfectly cold, filled the shell, added the Meringue and set it for a moment close under the front oven burner, turning until evenly browned. The pie tasted as though freshly baked, and the expense for GAS WAS SCARCELY ANYTHING [8]

CHOCOLATE SOUFFLE

3 ounces of chocolate
1 heaping tablespoonful of sugar
2 rounded tablespoonfuls of flour.
½ cupful of milk
Yolks of 3 eggs
Whites of 4 eggs
1 rounded tablespoonful of butter

Melt the butter in a small saucepan; stir into it the flour and let it cook a minute, but not brown, then add slowly the milk and stir until smooth and a little thickened; remove it from the fire and turn it slowly onto the yolks and sugar, which have been beaten to a cream; mix thoroughly and add the melted chocolate; stir for a few minutes, then set it away to cool; rub a little butter over the top so a crust will not form. When ready to serve, stir the mixture well to make it smooth and fold into it lightly the whites of the eggs, which have been whipped until very dry and firm. Turn the mixture into a buttered tin, filling it two thirds full. Have the tin lined with a strip of greased paper which rises above the sides to confine the souffle as it rises. Place the tin in a deep saucepan containing enough hot water to cover one half the tin. Cover the saucepan and place it where the water will simmer for thirty minutes, keeping it covered all the time. Place the tin on a very hot dish and serve at once. Cover the top with a hot tin until it reaches the diningroom if it has to be carried far.[16]

PENUCHE
Madeline G. Booth

2 cups light brown sugar, large piece butter, 1 cup granulated sugar, 1 teaspoon vanilla, salt, ¾ cup milk, ½ cup chopped walnuts. Cook sugar and milk until it thickens a little. Remove from fire and add butter, vanilla, and walnuts. Boil five to ten minutes.[11]

CARAMEL PRALINES
Jane Hoag

3 cups of sugar, 1 cup of milk, 1 tablespoon butter, 1 heaping cup pecan meats. Cook milk and 2½ cups sugar together. Melt the other ½ cup of sugar till it is brown, and when both are boiling, pour together. Let boil 5 minutes, or till it will form soft ball when dropped in cold water; add a pinch of salt. Remove from fire, add butter, beat till it begins to thicken. Add nuts and ½ teaspoon vanilla. Drop by tablespoon on oiled paper.[12]

MOLASSES CANDY
Madeline G. Booth

2 cups molasses, 2 level tablespoons butter, 2 cups brown sugar, ½ cup water, ¼ cup vinegar. Put all except vinegar into a large saucepan, and cook fast till a little of the mixture dropped into cold water feels brittle; add the vinegar, cook 2 minutes more and pour into a greased pan to cool. As soon as it can be easily handled, pull till white. Cut in pieces before it is too hard.[12]

Recognizing the Ladies' Room has been provided for their special use, where telephone, writing material, easy chairs, lavatory, etc. are to be found. This room makes a convenient place to meet a friend, or where a companion or children may wait comfortably while a depositor is attending to her banking business.[8]

APPLE FRITTERS
From the Kitchen of Brook Farm

Serves four, makes sixteen
2 eggs
½ cup milk
(Beat well (I use mixer). Sift together and add:
1 cup flour
1 tsp. baking powder
1 tsp. salt

Beat until smooth and set aside. Peel, core and slice ¼" thick rings of Golden Delicious or other apples. Heat vegetable oil in large skillet. Dip apple rings in batter and saute over medium heat until brown and puffed on both sides and apple is soft. You can do eight at a time in a 12" skillet. Drain well on paper towels. Sprinkle with sugar and cinnamon or plain granulated sugar and serve. You can keep these hot in a low oven for about half an hour.

CHOCOLATE BREAD PUDDING
Barbara Morey

3 slices white bread in small pieces
1 square bitter chocolate
1 tbsp. butter
pinch of salt
½ tsp. vanilla
¼ cup sugar
1 cup milk
1 egg well beaten

Put bread, chocolate, sugar, butter, salt and milk in sauce pan over low heat. Cook until chocolate is melted. Add egg and vanilla. Mix and pour into greased baking dish. Bake 350° for 25-30 minutes. Serve with a hard sauce made with 4 tbsp. butter and enough confectioner's sugar to make a sauce the consistency of whipped cream. Add 1 tsp. of vanilla.

BLUEBERRY DUMPLINGS
Edgar Taft

NOTE: This dessert will keep hot for 15-20 minutes in the covered pot and should be served hot. There is no salt and minimal sodium in this recipe. If desired, salt may be added to taste. Sweet margarine or salad oil may be substituted for butter. One level teaspoon baking powder with ⅓ cup skim milk or with ⅓ cup soy milk may be substituted for baking soda and buttermilk.

1 pint blueberries	¼ cup water
¼ cup sugar	1½ cups flour
3 tbsp. sweet butter	¼ cup sugar
⅓ tsp. baking soda	½ to ½ cup buttermilk

Pick over berries and bring to boil with water and sugar in flat bottomed pot with close-fitting lid at least 7 inches in diameter. Simmer for 3 to 4 minutes. Blend butter and flour sifted with sugar and baking soda until mixture resembles coarse corn meal. Stir in milk rapidly until just mixed. Drop by heaping teaspoonfuls into simmering berries. There should be enough dough for 6 dumplings. Cover and simmer for fifteen minutes. Serve dumplings with some of the blueberry sauce spooned over. Whipped cream may be served separately. Serves 6.

Blueberry dumplings were my grandmother's favorite dessert. The summer pudding (next page) really works though so much liquid seems to be involved. It is English country food, I guess. The dumplings certainly are New England.

Olive oil will remove gum from children's hair like magic.[3]

To Prevent Flies from Injuring Picture Frames, Etc. Boil three or four onions in a pint of water; then with a gilding brush do over your pictures and frames. The flies will not light on them. This may be used without apprehension, as it will not do the least injury to the frames.
  - Economical Housekeeper[1]

SUMMER PUDDING
Edgar Taft

1 qt. blueberries (raspberries, blackberries, currants)
¼ cup water
½ to ¾ cup sugar (or more to taste)
6-8 slices white bread with crusts cut off
Softened sweet butter, as needed

Lightly butter 4-5 cup bowl or pudding mold. Butter slices of bread and line mold, overlapping bread slices as necessary and reserving one or more slices sufficient to serve as a cover of the bowl or mold. Pick over berries and cook with water and sugar until soft—maximum 5 to 10 minutes. Pour cooked berries into lined bowl or mold. Cover berries with reserved bread and place a plate over all, weighted if necessary, to keep bread in place. Chill over night in refrigerator. Remove weight and plate and cover bowl or mold with serving plate. Invert and unmold onto serving plate. Serve with sweetened whipped cream. Serves 6.

PUMPKIN PEAR SAUCE PUDDING
Mary Seitz

Here is the way the Melville family might have used surplus pumpkins when they raised them during their sojourn at Arrowhead. This tradition was recently revived by Berkshire County Historical Society volunteers who ploughed, planted and harvested pumpkins in Arrowhead meadows for the benefit of museum preservation.

3 eggs
2 cups milk
1 teaspoon vanilla
1 teaspoon cinnamon (if not used in sauce)
⅛ teaspoon ginger
1 tablespoon butter

Preheat oven to 350°. Beat eggs, add liquids, then all other ingredients. Place in a 2 quart baking dish that is set in a pan of hot water. Bake about 1 hour until custard sets. Serves 6 to 8.

PUMPKIN PEAR SAUCE
Mary Seitz

Tester tried this with Anjou pears and found it much more interesting then with Red Bartletts. Bosc might be good too.

10 medium pears (or apples)
½ small pumpkin or 29 oz. can of Libby's)
½ cup sugar (or ¼ cup of honey)
2 tablespoons grated orange rind
1 teaspoon cinnamon
dash nutmeg

Wash fruit. Not necessary to peel them. Cut in chunks and remove seeds. Put in heavy pot with all other ingredients and cook over low heat until fruit is tender. Put through good grinder or blender and chill. Serve very cold.

EPILOGUE PUDDING DESSERT CONFECTIONS CONTEMPORARY SOURCES

VILLAGE INN TRIFLE
Clifford Rudisill

Cake:

1 cup sugar
6 egg yolks
¼ boiling water
¼ teaspoon salt
1 teaspoon vanilla extract
1 cup cake flour
1½ teaspoon baking powder
6 egg whites

Beat egg yolks until very light in color. Beat in sifted sugar and gradually beat in boiling water. Cool, then beat in vanilla extract.

Add sifted flour and baking powder to yolk mixture. Whip egg whites until stiff and fold in batter. Bake cake at 350° for about 45 minutes. Yield: One 9" cake. (To fill a traditional trifle dish, two cakes are required).

Custard:

¾ cup sugar
⅛ teaspoon salt
1 cup milk + 1 cup cream, mixed
4 egg yolks
1½ teaspoon vanilla extract
1 cup whipped cream, whipped
2 tablespoons butter
2 tablespoons cornstarch
4 egg yolks

Mix in top of double boiler: sugar, cornstarch and salt. Stir in milk and cream mixture. Cook covered for 8 minutes. Uncover and cook another 10 minutes. Add egg yolks, well beaten, and butter. Continue to cook and stir for two more minutes. Cool. Stir in vanilla extract. Fold in whipped cream. Chill.

To make two 9" cakes using above recipe: Cut cakes in half and sprinkle all four layers with medium-dry sherry, to taste. Spread tops of layers with a good quality strawberry preserve. Place thin layer of custard in bottom of traditional trifle dish, followed by a layer of sherry-soaked cake, and continue to alternate a layer of custard with a layer of cake, finishing with a layer of custard. Top with whipped cream and garnish with a few fresh strawberries.

VANILLA PUDDING WITH FRESH BERRIES AND RASPBERRY SAUCE
Anne Everest Wojtkowski

1 package of (4-serving size) vanilla pudding and pie filling
2 cups milk (to make pudding)
1 pint fresh raspberries
1 pint fresh strawberries, cleaned and halved
1 quart fresh blueberries, cleaned
raspberry syrup

Make pudding according to directions on package. Distribute it proportionately into four soup bowls, placing wax paper or plastic directly on its top to prevent film from forming. After pudding has cooled, remove wax paper or plastic. Proportionately distribute berries onto top of pudding. Drizzle syrup over the ingredients.
Note: Serve with ready-made or home made cookies. When I am in a rush, I especially favor Pepperidge Farm's "Champagne Assorted Cookies."

DELIGHT
Robert Cooper

16 oz. cottage cheese—low fat
1 - 6 oz. package jello (sugar free)
raspberries
strawberries
mandarin oranges
apricots
blueberries

Use your imagination. Coordinate Jello with whatever. Place cottage cheese in a large bowl. Sprinkle Jello over cheese. Add Cool Whip and mix. Add fruit and mix . . . (I like to break fruit up into tiny pieces.). Serve as salad (summer) or dessert.

MAPLE MOUSSE
Helen Plunkett

Beat three (3) egg whites stiff. Fold in one (1) pint of cream whipped stiff. Beat together: three (3) egg yolks, one half (½) cup sugar, one half (½) teaspoon vanilla. Fold into egg whites and cream mixture. Gently add—mixing well—one (1) cup of maple syrup or one (1) cup of chocolate syrup (Hershey's). Spoon into full cupcake containers and sprinkle with nuts of any kind. Put them in freezer.

BLUEBERRY CRISP
Jennifer Trainer

Fresh blueberries are sturdier than raspberries or blackberries and can be packed in a plastic container for each stowing. Mix the dry ingredients for the topping before leaving home. Keep the butter as cold as possible until time to blend it with the topping. If it is too soft, the texture of the topping will not be as good.

4 cups fresh blueberries
⅓ cup granulated sugar
¼ teaspoons grated lemon zest (optional)

Topping:
¾ cup all-purpose flour
¼ cup rolled oats
⅓ cup packed brown sugar
¼ teaspoon cinnamon
5 tablespoons unsalted butter (2½ ounces)
½ cup lightly toasted sliced almonds

Preheat the oven to 375°. Lightly butter a one quart baking dish. Mix the blueberries, sugar, and lemon zest in the baking dish and spread in an even layer.

To make the topping, mix the flour, oats, brown sugar, and cinnamon in a bowl. Cut the butter into small pieces and toss with the dry ingredients. With your fingertips, work in the butter until the mixture is crumbly. Add the almonds. Sprinkle the topping evenly over the blueberries. Bake for 30 to 40 minutes, until the top is golden brown and the juices are bubbling. Serve warm. Serves 4 to 6.[20]

CAROLE'S TARTS
Carole Owens
Comment: "From a group of party recipes I collected, invented, modified over the last thirty years—quick delicious, and pretty."

I.
1¼ cup graham cracker crumbs
6 tablespoons melted butter
3 tablespoons sugar

II.
1 pound cream cheese
1 teaspoon vanilla
½ cup sugar
2 eggs
1 teaspoon lemon juice

1. Combine ingredients I with fork and set aside.
2. Combine ingredients II in separate bowl (use blender).
3. Use small cupcake pan and papers. Fill each ¾ full using ⅓ graham cracker mixture topped with ⅔ cream cheese mixture.
4. Bake at 375° for 10 minutes.
5. Let cool and top with canned pie filling of choice—cherry, blueberry, etc.
6. Place on circular platter close together for color. If you use small enough cupcake papers, these can be eaten with fingers.

FINIS BEVERAGES OLD SOURCES

But a big dinner, with a hired chef and two borrowed footmen, with Roman punch, roses from Henderson's, and menus on gilt-edged cards, was a different affair, and not to be lightly undertaken. As Mrs. Archer remarked, the Roman punch made all the difference; not in itself but by its manifold implications—since it signified either canvasbacks or terrapin, two soups, a hot and a cold sweet, full decolietage with short sleeves, and guests of a proportionate importance.

EDITH WHARTON,
THE AGE OF INNOCENCE

A bar in modern style, well replenished with decanters, bottles, cigar boxes, and network bags of lemons, and provided with a beer entrance, an elderly person was smacking his lips with a zest which satisfied me that the cellars of the Province House still hold good liquor, though doubtless of other vintages than were quaffed by the old governors.

NATHANIEL HAWTHORNE,
HOWE'S MASQUERADE

GENERAL OBSERVATIONS ON BEVERAGES

Beverages are innumerable in their variety; but the ordinary beverages drunk in the British Isles, may be divided into three classes: 1. Beverages of the simplest kind not fermented. 2. Beverages, consisting of water, containing a considerable quantity of carbonic acid. 3. Beverages composed partly of fermented liquors. Of the first class may be mentioned,—water, toast-and-water, lemonade, orangeade, sherbet, apple and pear juice, capillaire, vinegar-and-water, raspberry vinegar and water.

Of the common class of beverages, consisting of water impregnated with carbonic acid gas, we may name soda-water, single and double ordinary effervescing draughts, and ginger-beer.

The beverages composed partly of fermented liquors, are hot spiced wines, bishop, egg-flip, ale posset, snack posset, punch, and spirits-and-water.

We will, however, forthwith treat on the most popular of our beverages, beginning with the one which makes "the cup that cheers but not inebriates."

The beverage called tea has now become almost a necessary of life. Previous to the middle of the 17th century it was not used in England, and was wholly unknown to the Greeks and Romans. Pepys says, in his Diary—"September 25th, 1661—I sent for a cup of tea (a China drink) of which I had never drunk before." [18]

TO MAKE A FINE SYLLABUB FROM THE COW

Sweeten a quart of cider with double refined sugar. Grate nutmeg into it. Then milk your cow into your liquor. When you have thus added what quantity of milk you think proper, pour a pint or more of the Sweetest cream you can get all over it.[1]

SWITCHEL
Barbara Pickett

Here is a somewhat early receipt from agrarian times.

1 gallon cold spring water	Variation:
2½ cups sugar	¼ cup maple syrup
1 cup 'ole time molasses	¼ cup vinegar
½ cup vinegar	¼ - ½ teaspoon ginger
⅔ teaspoon ginger	water to make 1 quart switchel

This combination of ingredients produced a thirst satisfying drink for men and boys when the sun was hot at hay harvesting time. It restored strength and quenched thirst.

BOILED COFFEE

Procure coffee freshly ground, one half Java and one half Mocca, and to one tablespoon for each person and one for the pot, add a little cold water, having first stirred the coffee with one beaten egg. Place upon the stove, and when hot, add the needed quantity of boiling water and let boil fifteen minutes. In every case, when serving, put cream and sugar into the cup before adding coffee. [16]

FRENCH WAY OF MAKING COFFEE

Put your coffee in the lower section of the top of a French coffee pot, and having placed upon the stove, pour boiling water, a little at a time, into the upper strainer, until you have the required quantity for the table. [9]

Substitutes for Tea and Coffee. The leaves of currant bushes picked very small and dried on tin can hardly be distinguished from green tea. Peas roasted and ground are an excellent substitute for coffee and you would hardly know which was best. [1]

Save all your fish skin, wash and dry it and keep to settle coffee. [1]

The best coffee is made by mixing the coffee with an egg and cold water -- allow this to boil three minutes. [3]

TO MAKE TEA

Black tea is more healthy and more cleanly than the green and requires more steeping. Allow one teaspoonful for each person, and one for the pot. Use an earthen tea-pot. The water should be boiling, but do not let the tea boil.[9]

TO MAKE COCOA

Ingredients: Allow 2 teaspoons of the prepared cocoa to 1 breakfast-cup; boiling milk and boiling water.
Mode: put the cocoa into a breakfast-cup, pour over it sufficient cold milk to make it into a smooth paste; then add equal quantities of boiling milk and boiling water, and stir all well together. Care must be taken not to allow the milk to get burnt, as it will entirely spoil the flavor of the preparation. The above directions are ususlly given for making the prepared cocoa. The rock cocoa, or that bought in a solid piece, should be scraped, and made in the same manner, taking care to rub down all the lumps before the boiling liquid is added.[9]

FROTHY CHOCOLATE

Put the milk upon the fire; when about, add the scraped chocolate, stir briskly for two minutes, then take from the fire and throw in with care a well-beaten egg.[9]

FRUIT JUICES

Grape Juice: Stem and wash grapes—cook fifteen minutes, drain in a cloth bag.[9]

MINT WATER

Steep two pounds of peppermint blossoms, with the yellow rinds of four lemons, in six quarts of alcohol, for eight days; distill in the waterbath; add a syrup made with nine pounds of sugar and three pints of water; to which is added half a pint of rose-water, and filter.

Peppermint-flowers, 2 lbs.; zests of lemons, 4; alcohol, 6 qts.; sugar, 9 lbs.; water, 3 pts.; rose-water ½ pt. Steep eight days.[11]

FILTERED WATER

It is a recognized fact that many diseases are contracted through drinking impure water, yet many are so careless as not to take the simple means of removing this danger. It only requires boiling the water to destroy the germs. This, however, does not remove the foreign matter, such as decayed vegetable growth and other substances, therefore it is well to filter as well as to boil water. Many good filters are made which are cheap and easy to clean. The Gate City Stone Filter is perhaps the simplest one, being an earthen crock with a porous stone bottom. Although all filters claim to remove germs as well as impurities from water, it is safer to boil it first. Bright, crystal-like water in clear glass carafes is an ornamental addition to the table service as well as a convenient way of serving it. If the carafes are stopped with cotton and placed in the refrigerator for several hours, the water will be refreshingly cool, and cracked ice, which many do not use, in the belief that it arrests digestion, will not be required.[16]

OXFORD NIGHTCAP

Take half a tumbler of tea, made as usual with sugar and milk, add a slice of lemon, a wine-glass of new milk, and the same of rum or brandy; beat up a new-laid egg, add to the whole while warm.[11]

Rose Water. Pick rose leaves when they are in full blossom. Put a peck of them to a quart of water in a cold still over a slow fire and distill very gradually. Bottle the water, let it stand three days and cork it close.[1]

If you spill coffee on your tablecloth, moisten with milk and rinse with warm water. The stain is all washed away and the cloth can be used again before going to the laundry.[9]

CARAWAY WATER

Macerate four ounces of pounded caraway-seeds in seven pints of alcohol for eight days; then distill in the water-bath, and add a syrup made with four pounds of sugar and three pints of water. Filter, and color green.

Caraway, 4 oz; alcohol, 7 pts.; sugar, 4 lbs.; water, 3 pts. Macerate eight days. [11]

CINNAMON WATER

Macerate two ounces of pounded cinnamon, ten drops of essence of lemon, and the yellow rind of two oranges, in seven quarts of alcohol, for eight days; then distill in the waterbath, and add a syrup made with eight pounds of sugar and two quarts of water. Color yellow.

Cinnamon, 2 oz.; essence of lemon, 10 drops; zests of orange, 2; alcohol, 7 qts.; sugar, 8 lbs.; water, 2 qts. Steep eight days. [11]

CLOVE WATER

Take one ounce of pounded cloves, one drachm of mace, seven pints of alcohol, and four pounds of sugar. Proceed as in Eau Divine, and color yellow. [11]

COWSLIP WINE

Ingredients To every gallon of water allow 3 lbs. of lump sugar, the rind of 2 lemons, the juice of 1, the rind and juice of 1 Seville orange, 1 gallon of cowslip pips. To every 4½ gallons of wine allow 1 bottle of brandy.

Mode Boil the sugar and water together for ½ hour, carefully removing all the scum as it rises. Pour this boiling liquor on the orange and lemon-rinds, and the juice, which should be strained; when milk-warm, add the cowslip pips or flowers, picked from the stalks and seeds; and 9 gallons of wine, 3 tablespoonfuls of good fresh brewers' yeast. Let it ferment 3 or 4 days; then put all together in a cask with the brandy, and let it remain for 2 months, when bottle it off for use.

Time To be boiled ½ hour; to ferment 3 or 4 days; to remain in the cask 2 months.

Average cost Exclusive of the cowslips, which may be picked in the fields, 2s. 9d. per gallon.

Seasonable Make this in April or May.[22]

COBBLERS

Put a claret-glassful of claret into a tumbler; add a teaspoonful of sugar, or sweeten to taste; fill the glass with ice cracked fine, and add a little water if desired. Place a shaker over the glass and mix it well; add a strawberry, raspberry, bit of pineapple, orange, or any fruit convenient; add also, two straws. Cobblers may be made of sherry, Catawba, or any wine, using a quantity in proportion to the strength desired. They are meant as light cooling drinks, and should not be strong of wine.[16]

ELDER WINE

Ingredients To every three gallons of water allow 1 peck of elderberries; to every gallon of juice allow 3 lbs. of sugar, ½ oz. of ground ginger, 6 cloves, 1 lb. of good Turkey raisins; ¼ pint of brandy to every gallon of wine. To every 9 gallons of wine 3 or 4 tablespoonfuls of fresh brewer's yeast.

Mode Pour the water, quite boiling, on the elderberries, which should be picked from the stalks, and let these stand covered for 24 hours; then strain the whole through a sieve or bag, breaking the fruit to express all the juices from it. Measure the liquor and to every gallon allow the above proportion of sugar. Boil the juice and sugar with the ginger, cloves, and raisins for 1 hour, skimming the liquor the whole time; let it stand until milk-warm, then put it into a clean dry cask, with 3 or 4 tablespoonfuls of good fresh yeast to every 9 gallons of wine. Let it ferment for about a fortnight; then add the brandy, bung up the cask, and let it stand some months before it is bottled, when it will be found excellent. A bunch of hops suspended to a string from the bung, some persons say, will preserve the wine good for several years. Elder wine is usually mulled, and served with sippets of toasted bread and a little grated nutmeg.[22]

MULLED WINE

To a pint of water put a teaspoonful of powdered cloves and cinnamon. Set it where it will boil—then separate the whites and yolks of three eggs, and beat the yolks with a large spoonful of powdered white sugar. As soon as the water boils, turn it on to the yolks and sugar—add a pint of wine, and turn the beaten whites of the eggs over the whole.[11]

ORANGE WINE

Take the expressed juice of eight Seville oranges; and having one gallon of water wherein three pounds of sugar have been boiled, boil the water and sugar for twenty minutes; skim constantly, and when cooled to a proper heat for fermentation, add the juice, and the outer rind of the fruit, shaved off. Put all into a barrel, stir it frequently for two or three days, and then closely bung it for six months before it is bottled.[11]

FLIP

Flips were originally hot drinks concocted in the winter and were warmed by thrusting an iron flip dog or loggerhead into the mug, which produced a pleasant sizzle and a burnt taste. Gradually they became cold drinks, and the flip dogs that hung by the fireplace were of no use except for poking large logs. A Yard of Flannel is not a Flip which, when properly made looks fleecy. In the eighteenth century, Myles Arnold reported the drink to be a favorite with the riders on the Boston Post route: "and indeed, 'tis said they sometimes wrap themselves warmly with it."[9]

TO MAKE A YARD OF FLANNEL

Heat 1 quart ale in a sauce pan. Beat 4 eggs with 4 tablespoons sugar and 1 teaspoon grated nutmeg or ginger, then add ½ cup dark rum. Pour into a pitcher. When ale is almost boiling, pour into another pitcher. To combine the two mixtures, pour hot ale, a little rum at a time, into egg mixture, stirring briskly to prevent curdling. Then, pour the contents of the two pitchers back and forth until the mixture is as smooth as cream.[9]

TO MAKE A COLD FLIP

Dissolve 1 teaspoon confectioner's sugar in a little water in a cocktail shaker. Add 1 jigger spirits or 2 jiggers wine, 1 egg, and 2 or 3 lumps of ice. Shake thoroughly and serve with a little grated nutmeg on top.

Barbara Allen (From the Berkshire County Historical Society Archives.)

BLACKBERRY CORDIAL

Squeeze the juice of ripe blackberries, and to every quart add one pound of loaf sugar; boil to a thin jelly, and to every quart add one pint of good brandy.[9]

RASPBERRY SHRUB

To five quarts red raspberries add one quart cider vinegar, and let it stand overnight. Squeeze through a cloth, then add five pounds of white sugar, boil five minutes and bottle. A little in a glass of ice water makes a delicious drink.[9]

BEER

For one-half barrel: one half pound hops, eight pounds of sugar, four quarts of corn, one pint of yeast.[9]

SPRING BEER
Clarissa Lathrop 1823 Pittsfield
Handwritten Recipe Book

Nettle roots, burdock and dandelion roots, butternut buds, birch bark, wintergreen, the bark of elder roots, red clover roots and tops, horseradish, black cherry bark, asparagus roots, sarsaparilla, white ash bark, the moss on barren moles, brook liver wort, cowslip roots and tops.

DRINK DIVINE

Mix a bottle of cider, half a bottle of perry, and the same of sherry, with half a gill of brandy, then add a sliced lemon, the rind pared as thin as possible, and a toasted biscuit, which is to be added to the liquor as hot as possible. Drink iced, or cooled.[11]

EGG FLIP

To make a quart of flip, put the ale on the fire to warm, and beat up three or four eggs with four ounces of moist sugar; remove the froth of the ale, while on the fire, until it begins to boil, mix the froth with the sugar and eggs, add grated nutmeg or ginger to taste, and a gill of rum. When the ale boils, stir it gradually into the eggs and rum, until quite smooth, then serve.[11]

FLAP

Put a little brandy in a tumbler, and add a bottle of soda-water.[11]

PARSNIP WINE

To 12 pounds of parsnips, cut in slices, add 4 gallons of water; boil them till they become quite soft. Squeeze the liquor well out of them. Run it through a sieve, and add to every gallon 3 pounds of loaf sugar. Boil the whole three quarts for an hour, and when it is nearly cold, add a little yeast. Let it stand for ten days in a tub, stirring it every day from the bottom, then put it into a cask for twelve months: as it works over, fill it up every day.[11]

EAU DIVINE

Macerate the zests of three limes and four lemons with four ounces of fresh orange-flowers, one ounce of fresh heads of balm, and six ounces of white hoarhound, in seven pints of alcohol, for ten days; distill in the water-bath, and add a syrup made with three pounds of sugar and one quart of distilled water.

Zests of orange, 12; neroli, 1 dr.; alcohol, 10 pts.; sugar, 4 lbs.; water, 1 qt. Steep fifteen days.[11]

MULLED WINE

1. Boil some cloves, mace, cinnamon, and nutmeg, in about a quarter of a pint of water till well flavored with spice, then add to a pint of port or home-made wine; sweeten to taste, and serve hot with thin toast or rusks.

2. Boil a small stick of cinnamon, a blade of mace, and three cloves, in a breakfastcupful of water for a few minutes; add some grated nutmeg and a pint of home-made or port wine, sweeten to taste, boil for one minute, and serve hot.

3. Put a bottle of port wine, half a bottle of water, and sugar to taste, into a saucepan, then add allspice, cloves, and a blade of mace; boil all together, serve in a jug with grated nutmeg, and rusks or slips of thin toast. Some persons add lemon-juice to the mull, but it does not generally please.[11]

GINGER BEER, INDIAN

To ten quarts of boiling water, add two ounces of pounded ginger, one ounce of cream of tartar, two limes, and two pounds of sugar. stir until cold, then strain through flannel until quite clear, adding a pint of beer, and four wine-glassfuls of good toddy. Bottle, tie down the corks, shake each bottle well for some time, place them upright, and they will be fit to drink the next day. This does not keep long.[11]

Iron Cement. Common wood ashes and salt, made into a paste with a little water, will quickly close a crack in a stove.[1]

A drop of peroxide of hydrogen will immediately remove a blood stain in a clean collar, gown or shirt.[2]

ORANGE WATER

Macerate the yellow rinds of a dozen oranges in ten pints of highly rectified spirits for fifteen days; add one drachm of neroli; distill in the water-bath and add a syrup made with four pounds of sugar and one quart of water, and filter.

Zests of orange, 12; neroli, 1 dr.; alcohol, 10 pts.; sugar, 4 lbs.; water 1 qt. Steep fifteen days.[11]

ROSEMARY WATER

Macerate eight ounces of rosemary blossoms in three pints of alcohol for ten days; then distill in the water-bath to perfect dryness.

Rosemary, 8 oz.; alcohol, 3 pts.[11]

TEA WATER

Distill one ounce of hyson and half an ounce of souchong tea in seven pints of alcohol by means of the water-bath; add a syrup made with two pounds of sugar and a quart of distilled water, and filter. This can also be made by infusion.

Hyson, 1 oz., souchong, ½ oz.; alcohol, 7 pts.; sugar, 2 lbs.; distilled water 1 qt.[11]

POSSET, COLD

Take a pint of cream, half a pint of white wine, the juice of half a lemon, and the peel rasped into it. Sweeten the cream and wine, put the latter into a basin, and then pour the cream from a height into the basin, stirring both well all the time; remove the froth, let it remain for a day in lukewarm water if the weather is cold, and then serve.[11]

FINIS BEVERAGES CONTEMPORARY SOURCES

HOT TOMATO DRINK
Janet Cook

6 cups tomato juice
1 can condensed consomme
1 teaspoon grated onion
1 teaspoon prepared horseradish
1 dash pepper
1 teaspoon Worcestershire sauce

Combine, heat. Stud lemon slices with cloves. Add to juice.

HOT & SPICY HOLIDAY CHEER
Carol Maynard

1 (46 oz.) can V-8 Juice
2 tablespoons brown sugar
2 tablespoons lemon juice
¼ teaspoon cinnamon
¼ teaspoon allspice
⅛ teaspoon ground cloves

Combine juice, brown sugar, lemon juice, spices in a stainless steel or enamel pan. Heat over medium heat until mixture just starts to simmer. Reduce heat to low and simmer 3 minutes. Serve in mugs or punch cups. May garnish with lemon slices and/or cinnamon sticks. May add a splash of vodka. To serve in quantities, keep in a crock pot and float lemon slices in it. Serves 12-18.

STRAWBERRY SMOOTHIE
Janet Cook

2 cups fresh strawberries
½ cup low fat plain yogurt
¼ cup low fat milk
2 envelopes aspartane
1 dash lemon bits

Blend in blender. Serve.

MULLED BEVERAGE MIX
Berkshire County Historical Society Archives

1½ cups water
¾ cup sugar
6 inches stick cinnamon, broken
6 whole cloves
Peel of ¼ lemon, cut into thin strips
½ cup lemon juice
Chilled or heated apple juice, cranberry juice cocktail, dry red or white wine, rose, or sparkling pink catawba juice.

In saucepan combine water, sugar, cinnamon, cloves and lemon peel. Bring to boiling, stirring till sugar is dissolved. Reduce heat; cover and simmer for 10 minutes. Stir in lemon juice. Strain through cheese cloth. Cover tightly and refrigerate as long as 6 weeks.

To serve, pour mix into a glass or mug and add desired beverage. Use two tablespoons mix to ¾ cup (6 ounces) beverage. (Serve chilled drink with ice if desired.) Garnish with orange slices and maraschino cherries on a skewer, if desired. Makes 1½ cups mix or enough for 12 servings.

ARROWHEAD PUNCH
(A non-alcoholic punch used at Arrowhead parties.)
BCHS Archives

To fill each punch bowl:
1. Dissolve 2 packages gelatin in 2 cups of boiling water.
2. Add 1 can (12 oz.) lemonade concentrate.
3. Add 6 cups cold water.
4. Add 1 large (64 oz.) bottle of cranberry juice.
5. Add at the last minute: 1 bottle ginger ale.

VINTAGE CAUTIONS & PRECAUTIONS

TO MAKE WHITE HAND SOAP

Save every scrap of fat each day; try out all that has accumulated, however small the quantity. This is done by placing the scraps in a frying-pan on the back of the range. If the heat is low, and the grease is not allowed to get hot enough to smoke or burn, there will be no odor from it. Turn the melted grease into lard-pails and keep them covered. When six pounds of fat have been obtained, turn it into a dish-pan; add a generous amount of hot water, and stand it on the range until the grease is entirely melted. Stir it well together; then stand it aside to cool. This is clarifying the grease. The clean grease will rise to the top, and when it has cooled can be taken off in a cake, and such impurities as have not settled in the water, can be scrapped off the bottom of the cake of fat.

Put the clean grease into the dish-pan and melt it. Put a can of Babbitt's lye in a lard-pail; add to it a quart of cold water, and stir it with a stick or wooden spoon until it is dissolved. It will get hot when the water is added; let it stand until it cools. Remove the melted grease from the fire, and pour in the lye slowly, stirring all the time. Add two tablespoonfuls of ammonia. Stir the mixture constantly for twenty minutes or half an hour, or until the soap begins to set.

Let it stand until perfectly hard; then cut it into square cakes. This makes a very good, white hard soap which will float on water. It is very little trouble to make.[16]

ORNAMENTS

Cut pretty, glittery ornaments from tin cans. Stars, icicles, snow flakes, even angel wings can be cut out with a pair of tin snips and a bit of imagination. Cover with bright paper the cardboard frames you find inside a ball of darning cotton or crochet cotton. Also use small face powder boxes as forms. There are dozens of such forms that can be used—toilet tissue rolls make pretty candles, etc. Attach wire or string so that the ornament can be hung on the tree.[3]

HOW TO STONE OLIVES

With a sharp-pointed knife, cut through the olive to the stone on the blossom end and pare off the meat, turning the olive around three times, keeping the knife at not too sharp an angle close to the stone. The meat will then be in one curled piece, which can be pressed into its original shape again.[16]

TO KEEP BUTTER

To have sweet butter in dog days and through the vegetable seasons, send stone pots to honest, neat dairy people, and procure it packed down in May, and let them be brought in in the night or cool rainy mornings, and partake of no heat from the horse, and set the pots in the coldest part of cellar.[1]

That worn-in-the-middle sheet is good for something! Just hem, as you would any curtain, trim with braid, fringe, etc. and you will be surprised how pretty the old sheet will look at your window.[3]

Put your lace away in blue tissue paper if you wish it to retain its whiteness. In mending lace curtains, dampen a piece of new with thin-starch: draw the rent carefully together. Place net over it and press dry with warm iron.[8]

Camphor gum will keep silver from tarnishing. Put a piece in paper and lay in box with silver.[8]

A simple polish for raw furniture can be made of one part turpentine and three parts linseed oil in a few drops of vinegar. Some rules give only two parts of oil to one of turpentine.[8]

Do not be afraid to wash your piano with soft warm water and wipe dry with a chamois.[8]

The odor of tobacco smoke can be removed by placing a large bowl of fresh water in the room over night.[8]

Use oil of cedar occasionally about your closets, and you will not be troubled with moths. Put a few drops on a cloth and rub in corners under shelves, etc. In putting away furs or woolen clothes, a little of the oil dropped on a piece of cotton and placed in box, is desirable.[8]

A FEW THINGS KEROSENE WILL DO.

For ants, saturate rags with kerosene and hang or lay these near their runs and they will quickly disappear. For cleaning painted and varnished woodwork, painted walls, varnished floors, bath tubs and marble washstands it is unsurpassed. For tubs and marble, apply with a woolen cloth, then wash with soap and water. For woodwork and walls, use clean cloths, changing as soon as soiled. A few drops in the water when washing windows and mirrors will give them a beautiful polish.[8]

Grease spots in cloth may be taken out by applying a solution of salt in alcohol.[8]

To remove tar or pitch; rub well with lard, then wash in soap and hot water; treat wheel grease in same way.[8]

A weak solution of oxalic acid, labeled and kept on the sink shelf, is useful for removing stains from the hands.[8]

MATCH MARKS

Marks that have been made on paint with matches can be removed by rubbing first with a slice of lemon, then with whiting, and washing with soap and water.[8]

TO CLEAN BRASS

Clean it with pulverized pumice stone wet with household ammonia; applying this paste first and polishing the brass when this has dried, suing for this purpose chamois skin. Wring out a flannel cloth in kerosene. Rub upon pulverized pomade, clean the brasses and polish with old linen.[8]

When a blue serge suit gets shiny, make a solution of warm water and borax, one tablespoonful to each quart of water. Rub the shiny spots and press while damp.[3]

A drop of peroxide of hydrogen will immediately remove a blood stain in a clean collar, gown or shirt.[12]

SHOE BLACKING

Wash elderberries in a kettle of water. Set them in the shade for a day or two to ferment, then boil it half a day, adding a little water as needed. Strain the liquid and boil it down to the thickness of molasses. It will give a fine gloss with rubbing.

Good writing ink can be made the same way.

CAUTIONS

ACCIDENTS BY FIRE If females and children must wear cotton and linen dresses and aprons in winter, use the precaution to dip the dresses in strong alum water, after washing. This will prevent blazing if they catch fire. In nurseries there ought to be provided strong sacks, three and a half feet in depth, and one and one-half in diameter, kept open at the top with a thick wooden hoop, having a long rope fastened to it. Into these sacks, should an unhappy accident require it, the children may be put and let down.[1]

HANNAH BARNARDS SALVE FOR BURNS

Diaries & Writings of Clarissa Lathrop

Take two ounces of burgundy pitch, add half an ounce bees-wax. Add to that quantity an even tablespoonful of hogs lard or any oily substance to render it sufficently soft but not so as to melt with the warmth of the flesh. Spread it on an old napkin or any other fine clean soft cloth.
BCHS Archives - Jabez Lane Family Papers

SYRUP FOR THE SPRING OF THE YEAR

Boil together, dock root, thoroughwort, yarrow, mullein, sarsaparilla, coltsfoot, spearmint, May weed, dandelion root, and any other herbs you like. Boil down the water and add molasses to make a syrup. Put in brandy to keep. Make a good deal of this, and give all the family a tablespoonful before breakfast as a prevention of Spring fevers.[1]

FOOD

Add a tablespoonful of minute tapioca to the filling of a fruit pie, it helps retain the juice and improves the consistency.[12]

For a change make a thin custard and serve with jello. It is a change from whipped cream. Flavor with vanilla.[12]

When cooking rhubarb add a pinch of soda and then it only takes half as much sugar.[12]

HEALTH HELPS

By observing the following few and simple Rules, better health may be expected than from the use of the most powerful medicines:
1. Avoid as much as possible living near a graveyard.
2. Avoid too plentiful Meals.
3. Shun the night air as you would the Plague.[1]

For a sudden attack of Quinsy or Croup, or a cold that is tight on the lungs, bathe the neck with bear's grease and pour it down the throat. Goose grease or any kind of oil grease is as good as bear's grease. Onions stewed in molasses are loosening. Put draughts of wilted horseradish leaves on the feet. A drop or two of skunk's oil or hen's oil on a lump of sugar will loosen up a cold.[1]

FOR AN ORDINARY HEADACHE

Take a shovel full of clean wood ashes; put them into clear cold water. When it has settled drink the water. It may cause vomiting; if it does the headache will be relived sooner.[1]

FOR EARACHE

Soak the feet in warm water; roast an onion and put the heart of it into the ear as hot as can be borne and bind roasted onions on the feet.[1]

OTHER CURES FOR CONSUMPTION

Take no food but new Buttermilk churned in a Bottle and white bread. I have known this successful. Or, every morning cut a little turf of fresh Earth, and lying down breathe into the hole for a quarter of an hour.[1]

To prevent wounds from mortifying, sprinkle sugar on them and it will prevent it.[1]

SIMPLE REMEDY FOR COUGHS

Pour 1 pint boiling water over 1 tablespoon whole flax seed in a bowl. Place bowl over boiling teakettle for ½ hour. Strain, and add juice of ½ lemon and sugar to sweeten. One or two swallows of this may be taken frequently while cough lasts.[12]

SIMPLE HEADACHE CURE

Take a quantity of black pepper and put it in a handkerchief; then fold the handkerchief over so that the grains cannot fall out, and saturate the whole thing with camphor.[8]

CHAPPED HANDS

One ounce alcohol, one ounce glycerine, one ounce cologne, one ounce tarsgacanth. Dissolve the last in a little water, then add hot water: when dissolved and hot add other ingredients.[8]

FOR A SEVERE COLD

Do not eat a morsel of anything for twenty-four or thirty-six hours; taste not even a sip of milk, as this sets the human machinery to work and adds fuel to the already overheated system. Drink water, fresh and moderately heated; do not boil it. Drink a glass or two every hour during the day; mind, a glass; do not try to drink it from a cup. You will get over it in the soonest possible time.[8]

FOR TOOTHACHE

Of powdered alum and fine salt, equal quantities; apply to the tooth and it will speed relief.[1]

BIBLIOGRAPHY

1. *Pocumtuc Housewife, A Guide to Domestic Cookery*; Womens Alliance of First Church, Deerfield, Massachusetts. Printed 1897 based on 1805 sources.
2. *The New Cookbook*; Ladies of Congregational Church, Adams, Massachusetts. Adams Freeman Book and Job Print, Adams, Massachusetts 1887.
3. *Service League Cookbook*; First Congregational Church, Stockbridge, Massachusetts 1948.
4. *The Table*; Alessandro Filippini, Charles L. Webster & Co., New York 1889. Hopper McGraw & Co., Baltimore 1891.
5. *Mrs. E. H. Marsh's Recipe Book*; (Hand crafted) 1858.
6. *Mrs. Lincoln's Boston Cookbook*; Mrs. D. A. Lincoln, Roberts Bros., Boston, Massachusetts 1896.
7. *Sandisfield Cookery*; Sandisfield Historical Society, K & R Printing Co., Ellington, Connecticut 1976.
8. *North Adams Cookbook*; Women of the City, Walden and Crawly Printers, North Adams, Massachusetts 1905.
9. *South Church Cook Book*; Chickering & Axtell Steam Printers, Pittsfield, Massachusetts 1887.
10. *The Complete Hostess*; Dorcas Class, South Congregational Church, Pittsfield, Massachusetts (No Date).
11. *Early American Beverages*; John Hull Brown, Bonanza Books, New York 1966.
12. *Cook Book*; First Methodist Episcopal Church, Pittsfield, Massachusetts 1926.
13. *Bicentenniel Cookbook*; Compiled by Madelaine Brown 1767-1967. Lenox, Massachusetts 1967.
14. *Recommended Receipts*; Busy Bees, 1928.
15. *Berkshire County WCTU Cook Book*; Berkshire Courier Print, Great Barrington, Massachusetts 1899.
16. *Century Cookbook*; The Century Company, De Venna Press, Glenville, New York 1895.
17. *Best of Shaker Cooking*; Miller & Fuller, Eagle Publishing Co., Pittsfield, Massachusetts 1985.
18. *Mrs. Beeton's Book of Household Management*; By Law & Brydon. Thetford Norfolk, Great Britain 1859-1861.
19. *Food from Heartland*; Glenn Andrews, Prentice Hall Press, New York 1991.
20. *Yachting Cookbook*; Jennifer Trainer and Elizabeth Wheeler, Bantam Press, New York 1990.
21. *From Monastery Garden*; Boulding, Harper & Rowe, New York, New York 1976

BCHS COOKBOOK COMMITTEE

Bythe Randolph
Carolyn E. Banfield

Molly Geraghty
Cliff Rudisill
Audrey Sweeney
Janet Cook

Bibliography

BCHS Board Members

Berkshire Victuals could not have become a reality without the publication expertise of Carolyn E. Banfield, and the technical skills of Stella Coolbroth. Sincere thanks to both.